CREATING A
Web Site
by Greg Rickaby

WILEY

CREATING A WEB SITE

Published by: **John Wiley & Sons, Inc.,** 111 River Street, Hoboken, NJ 07030-5774, www.wiley.com

Copyright © 2017 by John Wiley & Sons, Inc., Hoboken, New Jersey

Media and software compilation copyright © 2017 by John Wiley & Sons, Inc. All rights reserved.

Published simultaneously in Canada

For general information on our other products and services, please contact our Customer Care Department within the U.S. at 877-762-2974, outside the U.S. at 317-572-3993, or fax 317-572-4002. For technical support, please visit https://hub.wiley.com/community/support/dummies.

Wiley publishes in a variety of print and electronic formats and by print-on-demand. Some material included with standard print versions of this book may not be included in e-books or in print-on-demand. If this book refers to media such as a CD or DVD that is not included in the version you purchased, you may download this material at http://booksupport.wiley.com. For more information about Wiley products, visit www.wiley.com.

Library of Congress Control Number is available from the publisher

ISBN: 978-1-119-37651-4

ISBN 978-1-119-37652-1 (ebk); ISBN 978-1-119-37653-8 (ebk)

Manufactured in the United States of America

10 9 8 7 6 5 4 3 2 1

CONTENTS

PROJECT 6: MAKE YOUR WEB SITE LOOK GREAT 93

INTRODUCTION

WELCOME TO HOW TO CREATE A WEB SITE! Web sites have many different purposes, ranging from a small personal web site, to a large e-commerce (shopping) web site, or even a social network web site with billions of users.

So what is a web site, anyway? Many web sites are written in three different programming languages named HTML, CSS, and JavaScript. When you put all three of those languages together, they form a web page. When you put several web pages together under a single domain name, you can create a web site.

ABOUT THIS BOOK

In this book, you learn how to build your very own web site. There are a few items you will need in order to become a junior webmaster:

» A computer running a modern version of Windows, Mac OS, or Ubuntu operating system

» A reasonably fast Internet connection

» A modern web browser, such as Google Chrome or Mozilla Firefox

» A Google (Gmail) account

» A plain old pencil and paper

As you work through each project, keep in mind the following writing conventions:

Code and web addresses are in `monofont`. If you're reading this as an e-book, you can click web addresses like http://www.dummies.com/ to visit that web site.

A WORD ABOUT COPYRIGHT

What is copyright? It means that someone has created a "thing" and only that person is allowed to use that "thing" unless the person gives permission to someone else who asked for it.

Luckily there are people and organizations who enjoy sharing their work. Photographs that are allowed to be shared (or redistributed) are usually licensed under the *Creative Commons Zero* (https://creativecommons.org/).

Some computer and web software is free under a license called "General Public License" (or GPL for short). This software is called "open source," meaning that anyone can use or manipulate the source code any way he or she wants.

Copyright and intellectual property law is a serious issue and there are legal consequences for using other people's work without their permission. I encourage you to read more about copyright on Wikipedia (https://en.wikipedia.org/wiki/Copyright). I also ask that if you use a photo, video, or text from another web site, you list your sources (just be sure you are allowed borrow this content!) either in the footer or on a special page on your web site. If you have any questions about copyright, ask an adult to help you find out more.

ABOUT YOU

Every junior webmaster needs to start somewhere, but this book assumes that you have the ability to

» Type on a computer, use a mouse, and follow directions.

» Have an email address and Google account. Several of the projects in this book require you to sign up for a (free) account to access services and tools. Please get an adult's permission first!

» Not be afraid to fail. Nobody is perfect, and not a single person became a web professional without first making (lots of) mistakes.

Finally, spelling and formatting is important. Computers are really powerful, but they are actually pretty dumb and very picky about how their instructions are written. If a computer can't understand a command, it won't know what to do and nothing will happen. You may need to spend some extra time working through spelling and formatting errors.

ABOUT THE ICONS

As you read through the projects in this book, you'll see a few icons. The icons point out different things:

This icon points out tips that can make your projects run more smoothly.

This icon alerts you to information that you'll want to remember.

This icon marks important information that you can use to avoid common pitfalls when coding.

FURTHER READING

Some of the concepts for writing code are covered in another book written for kids like you: *Getting Started with Coding,* by Camilla McCue, and *Writing Computer Code,* by Chris Minnick and Eva Holland.

You are going to be learning a lot about Google Drive, programming languages, and being creative. I recommend that you seek help from online tutorials, YouTube videos, and web sites such as www.w3schools.com or thewecan.zone/website-building any time you get stuck. And don't ever be afraid to ask for help from a parent or friend! The best webmasters are ones who talk with other people.

PROJECT 1 CHOOSE A TOPIC

FINDING A SINGLE TOPIC OR IDEA FOR YOUR WEB SITE TO FOCUS ON CAN BE DIFFICULT. In fact, it can be the single most difficult part of building a web site. Inspiration is a funny thing; it can come from anywhere and nowhere! Sometimes coming up with a topic can take days or weeks.

Don't be discouraged if you can't choose something quickly. You don't want to create a web site about a topic that really doesn't interest you, only to then feel that you have to stick with it. To help you avoid that situation, here are some techniques to focus your energy on just one topic.

BUILD A WORD CLOUD

Grab a pencil and notepad and start writing down your favorite things to do. If you're really into Pokémon, go ahead and write that down. If you enjoy studying dinosaurs, write that down, too.

Do you participate in extracurricular activates such as karate class, ballet, or soccer, or maybe you can play an instrument? Having experience with a particular topic provides a solid foundation that makes creating fun and engaging content easier.

Think of what you talk about with your friends. My son is into Pokémon, and I am sure he could speak for days about his favorite characters. Is there a certain cartoon character or superhero that you love? If so, you could create a web site dedicated to Captain America or Spider-Man, for example.

The ideas can be about anything! The important thing is to just start writing them on paper. If you can, try to come up with at least ten topics, as shown in the following figure:

Website Topics

Cartoons
Legos
*Dinosaurs ... Carnivores
Pokémon   T-Rex | Raptor
Wrestling
Making Videos
Disney movies ... ~~Princesses~~
Drawings
Funny stories
Jokes
KARATE
* Star Wars ... BB8?
                 ↓
Painting   Types of Droids
Reptiles
Storms

Remember, there are no wrong ideas. The goal is to have as many topics on paper as possible!

LOOK AT SIMILAR WEB SITES

If you're still having trouble coming up with a topic, why not take a look around the Internet at what others are doing? You'd be surprised how often I still get inspired by looking at how other people have designed their web site.

HOW TO BE SAFE WHILE SURFING THE WEB

There are a few things you should know before getting online. Some of these rules even apply to adults!

1 **Never give anyone personal information about yourself, such as your name, address, phone number, or location.**

2 **If you see anything inappropriate that makes you feel scared, sad, confused, or uncomfortable, tell an adult immediately.**

3 **Get permission from an adult before posting photos or videos to web sites, emails, or chat rooms.**

4 **Never download files onto your computer without help from an adult.**

5 **Do not be rude or bully anyone online.**

6 **Never meet anyone face to face that you met on the Internet, unless you tell an adult who will go with you.**

7 **Ask an adult to install an ad-blocking browser extension such as *uBlock Origin (https://www.ublock.org)* or *AdBlock Plus (https://adblockplus.org)*. These tools can help make surfing safer by blocking unwanted advertisements and pop-ups, and by stopping suspicious scripts.**

Always keep in mind that on the Internet, people can easily pretend to be someone they're not. So be always be cautious, and if you don't know, ask an adult!

HOW TO SEARCH WITH GOOGLE.COM

Follow these steps to perform a search on Google:

1 Open a web browser.

A web browser is an application that lets you search the Internet and visit web sites. Common web browsers are Microsoft Edge, Google Chrome, Mozilla Firefox, and Safari. Which one do you use on your computer?

2 In the address bar, type https://google.com/ **and then press Enter.**

A search box appears near the middle of the Google home page.

3 Type search words in the search box.

If you wanted to create a web site about dinosaurs, you could type **dinosaurs** in this box. Google automatically performs a search and displays results immediately.

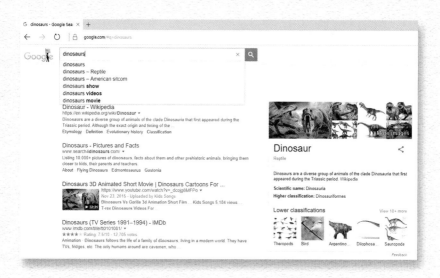

4 Click the blue-colored links to view the web site.

While you are looking at other web sites for inspiration; pay close attention to their layout, the colors, photos, and content. You might just stumble upon something that you might want to use on your web site. Think about how could you do it similarly — but without copying that web site.

HOW TO SEARCH USING SIMILARSITES.COM

Another great resource for finding topics is a web site service called *Similar Sites*. Much like Google, it is a search engine that helps you find web sites that contain similar information.

1 Open a web browser.

By now, you should know how to open a web browser and enter web addresses. If you still need help from an adult, don't worry! It just takes a little practice.

2 **In the address bar, type** http://similarsites.com/ **and then press Enter.**

In the middle of the home page, you see a large search box.

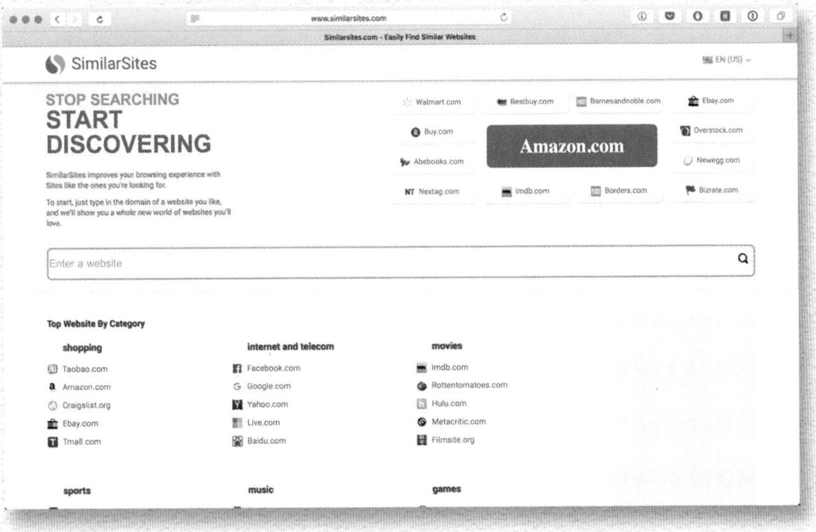

3 **In the search box, type the topic or idea (such as** dinosaurs) **and press Enter.**

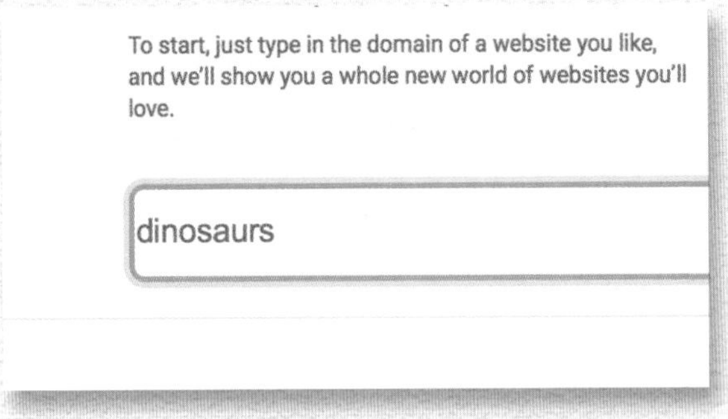

To start, just type in the domain of a website you like, and we'll show you a whole new world of websites you'll love.

> dinosaurs

You see a list of web sites. Click the results to view the web site.

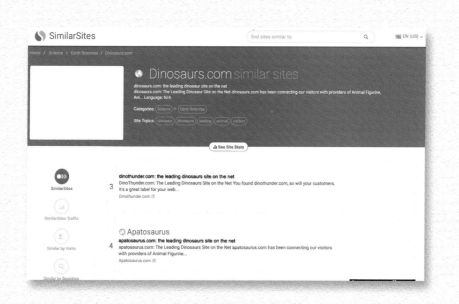

SEARCH OFFLINE

You can also look at magazines to get ideas for your web site. Does anything on the cover stand out? Or perhaps you have a favorite book that might cover a topic that you love. You might also want to visit your local library to search for ideas.

ELIMINATE WEAK IDEAS

By now, you should have a few ideas on paper. Look for the ones you don't feel as strongly about. Some good questions to ask are "Could I write about this topic at length?" and "In a few months, am I still going to want to write or talk about this?"

The goal is to trim down the list to just one idea, so if you cannot definitely say "yes" to a topic, cross it off the list.

~~Everything~~
~~Making videos~~
~~Dinosaur movies~~ ... ~~Princesses~~
~~Drawings~~
Funny stories

DECIDE WHOM YOU WANT TO TALK TO

Almost as important as the topic is deciding whom you want to reach as an audience. Do you want to create a web site for your family? Maybe classmates or teammates? If you're writing content about dinosaurs for your classmates, think about how you would explain information to them in person.

Talking to your friends about your topic can really help you narrow down your ideas. It can also help you come up with some of your content!

If your topic interests only you, it is probably not worth writing about. A good web site keeps the reader in mind at all times. This often means choosing topics that haven't been written about too much, and maybe choosing a more current topic.

Don't be afraid to ask an adult for help with ideas. Chances are, an adult you're close to has had to find a topic for a school or college essay. I'm sure that an adult in your life would love to help you figure out your topic.

PROJECT 2 CREATE A SITE MAP

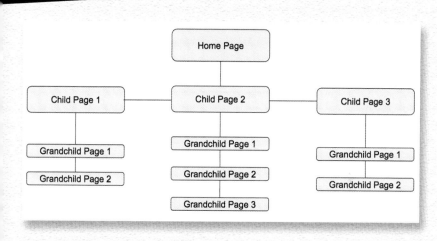

WHAT EXACTLY IS A SITE MAP? Just as a regular ol' map will help you find your way, a site map helps search engines, like Google, find their way around your web site. A site map can also be a document for displaying a list of pages in a web site. In this project, you will learn how to create a site map, which will help you think about how you want to structure your content.

DECIDE HOW YOU WANT TO LAY OUT YOUR CONTENT

Now that you have a topic, it's time to focus on how you want to lay it out. Web sites all have a home page, which is a great place to start your site map. For example, if you are creating a web site about dinosaurs, here are some pages and sections you might see:

Home Page

Dinosaur Timeline

Jurassic Area

Triassic Area

> Dinosaur Types
>
> Carnivore
>
> Herbivore
>
> Omnivore
>
> Dinosaur Names
>
> Stegosaurus
>
> Tyrannosaurus

Knowing how you want this content laid out before you start on the actual pages will really help!

CREATE A SITE MAP WITH GOOGLE DRAWINGS

In the Introduction, I mention that you need to have a Google account. If you don't have an account, grab an adult to help you log in to Google to create one. (By law, you must be at least 13 years old to create any online account.)

If you can't use Google Drawings, follow along anyway. You can apply the same concepts by using a pencil and paper.

CREATE A NEW GOOGLE DRAWINGS DOCUMENT

1 **Open a web browser.**

2 **In the address bar, type** https://docs.google.com/drawings/ **and press Enter.**

If you're logged in to Google, you should see a screen similar to the one in the following figure.

3 In the top left, click the words *Untitled drawing*.

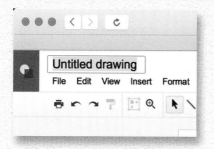

4 Type a name for your drawing and press Enter to save the title.

For this example, I name the drawing Dinosaur Website Site Map.

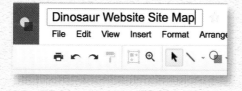

Now you can start choosing how to lay out content bubbles. To do so, you need the topic you came up with in Project 1.

DRAW YOUR FIRST CONTENT BUBBLE IN GOOGLE DRAWINGS

With your topic handy, you need to start creating content bubbles. You use these bubbles to represent sections of your web site.

With Google Drawings, you don't need to click Save because Google Drawings automatically saves the document anytime a change is made.

1 **Click the Shape icon.**

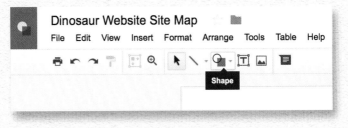

2 **Move your mouse cursor down and to the right and choose a style.**

I personally prefer the Rounded Rectangle the best, but you can choose whichever shape you like best.

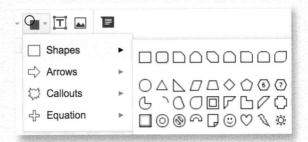

Great job! Now you can start creating content bubbles with your mouse. Remember that you should start with the most important page on your web site: the home page.

3 The area below the toolbar (with the gray- and white-shaded boxes) is called the canvas. Place your mouse cursor near the top and middle of the canvas. Click and hold down your mouse button and move to the right to draw a shape.

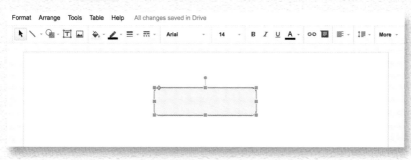

4 Double-click the shape again to activate the Text tool.

5 Type Home Page and then click anywhere in the canvas to save.

The home page is always the parent page. Additional pages are called child *pages. Any additional pages below a child page are called* grandchild *pages. When you assemble your pages in this order, you're putting them in a hierarchy (a rank), with the most important pages at the top.*

CREATE ADDITIONAL CONTENT BUBBLES

After you create a content bubble for the home page, you can simply duplicate the home page bubble for each additional page you want to create. You can also draw a line to connect the home page with each child page.

1 **Select the content bubble and then click Edit and select Duplicate.**

The bubble automatically gets copied, or duplicated. (You can also use a keyboard shortcut: Just click ⌘-D on a Mac or Ctrl+D on a PC.)

2 **Move the bubble right below the Home Page bubble.**

3 **Click inside the bubble. Type the name of your first child page.**

4 **Move your mouse back to the menu bar. Click the icon with the diagonal line. Select the Line tool.**

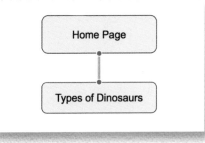

5 **Move your mouse cursor to the home page bubble. Click the bottom of the bubble. A purple dot should appear.**

6 **From the purple dot, click and drag your mouse straight down to connect the purple dot to the bubble right below.**

Very good! You've just connected two pieces of content and created your very first site map! To create additional content bubbles, you will need to repeat Steps 1–6.

For example, if you create a page called Types of Dinosaurs, you can create bubbles for child pages related to that topic (called Carnivore, Herbivore, and Omnivore, for example) and place them directly underneath. Then use the Line tool again to connect the pages. (Do this for your own topic, of course; the figure is just an example.)

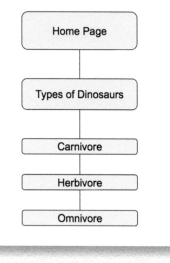

Great! Now you have a basic site map that contains pages in the order of parent, child, and grandchild (hierarchical) order.

Continue to repeat Steps 1–6 for each page you want to create for your topic. When you finish, you might have a site map that looks similar to the following:

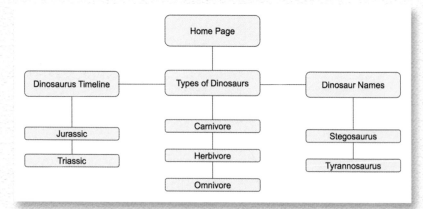

Be patient! It may take a little while to get everything just right, but when you're done, you'll have a clear direction on how your content should be displayed. This process helps you stay focused when you work through the other projects in this book.

DRAW A SITE MAP USING A PENCIL AND PAPER

Drawing a site map on paper rather than in Google Drawings is perfectly okay, too! In fact, you might find it easier to draw it out on paper first and then make a digital copy for easy reference later.

1 **Find a blank piece of paper and a pencil.**

2 **Turn the paper sideways.**

3 **At the top, write the name of your web site.**

   For this project's example, it's Dinosaur Website Site Map.

4 **Draw a rectangular content bubble shape near the top and in the middle.**

5 **Write** Home Page **in the middle of the content bubble.**

6 **Draw another content bubble directly below, leaving just enough space to draw a straight line.**

7 **Write the name of your first child page.**

   For this project's example, one is Types of Dinos.

8 **Draw a line from the Home Page bubble to the child page bubble.**

Awesome! You've certainly got the idea now! Repeat Steps 4–8 until you've drawn content bubbles for each of your pages.

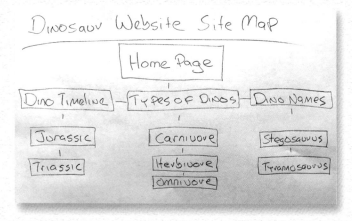

By now, you should have a completed site map.

You will need to reference this site map later on, so make sure to keep it handy. You can use a hand-drawn copy, a printed one, or a copy that you keep open in a browser tab from Google Drawings. Now that you have a site map, you are ready for Project 3! Excellent!

PROJECT 3 CREATE A WIREFRAME

Logo		Menu Item	Menu Item	Menu Item

		Featured Dinosaur
	Dino Image	Dino Facts Widget
		Dino Quiz Widget

Footer

YOU KNOW YOUR FINISHED WEB SITE IS GOING TO LOOK GREAT. After all, with all your exciting graphics and videos, why wouldn't it? To make sure that your web site lives up to your dreams and has room for all your content, you need to have a plan. In this project, you figure out the initial layout for your web site.

WHAT IS A WIREFRAME?

A *wireframe* is like a blueprint for a web site. It helps you figure out just where to put all your content, graphics, videos, and other elements on a page.

Usually, wireframes are presented in two formats:

» **Low-fidelity:** These wireframes are just rough sketches or doodles.

» **High-fidelity:** These wireframes can represent the final design, showing each section in greater detail.

Typically, a web site has a header, body, sidebar, and footer. The layout of a web site, of course, can be anything the web site creator wants it to be, but most people who look at web sites have come to expect content to be laid out as shown in the figure.

When you create your wireframe, you may want to model this layout.

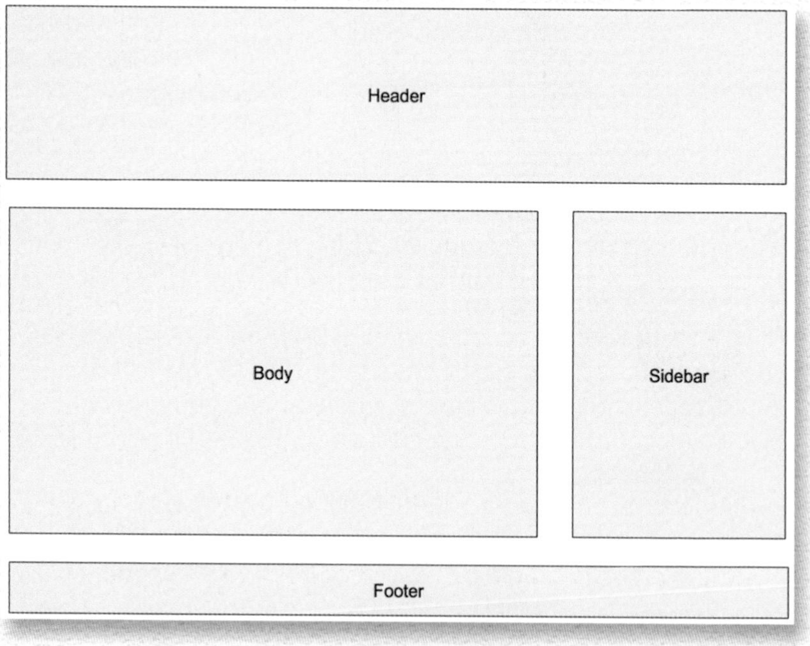

Header

Body

Sidebar

Footer

THE BASICS: WHAT YOU NEED TO KNOW TO GET STARTED

Before you dive in and create your web site, sketch a drawing of how you want your web site to look.

You can draw your wireframe on paper or make one using your favorite drawing app, such as Google Drawings.

Of course, the one shown here is just an example. You can draw your wireframe any way you want. Be as creative as you like!

No matter how you decide to create your low-fidelity wireframe, keep in mind that you're using straight lines and basic drawings for photos and videos. The goal is to imagine what your web site layout might be.

Right now, focus on where the logo, menu, body content, and footer are going to go. Don't be afraid to scratch stuff out and start over. You don't need to worry about colors or fonts in this project!

CREATE A LOW-FIDELITY WIREFRAME

In Project 2, you learn how to make a site map with Google Drawings. In this project, you use the same tool to create your first wireframe.

If you don't have access to Google Drawings, you can still follow along. Just grab a pencil and paper and do each step on paper instead of the computer.

It's okay if the wireframe doesn't look much like a web site. The goal is to simply get your ideas sketched out and then improve on them!

For this project, you need to have your site map from Project 2. Open the site map in your web browser, or print it. (Go back to Project 2 and create a site map, if you haven't already.)

PLACE THE LOGO

With your site map handy, follow these steps to create a low-fidelity wireframe:

1 **On your web browser, go to https://docs.google.com/ drawings and open Google Drawings.**

2 **For the logo, draw a rectangle.**

You can draw a rectangle by clicking the Shape tool icon, choosing Shapes, and then selecting Rectangle.

3 Place the rectangle near the top left of the screen.

You can place this logo anywhere you'd like, but most web sites put their logo in the top-left area, which is called the *header*.

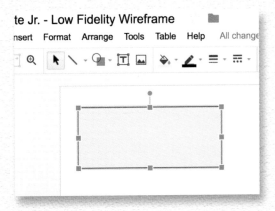

4 Double-click the center of your logo rectangle.

The text tool appears.

5 Type Logo.

6 Finish by clicking off to the left in the blank space.

CREATE THE NAVIGATION MENU

Most web sites put their navigation menu near the top of the wireframe as well. You could place navigation next to the logo or below it.

To create the navigation menu:

1 **Draw a smaller rectangle and place it near the middle of the header.**

> Logo

2 **Duplicate this menu item a few times and place these rectangles next to each other. In the menu bar, click Edit and then click Duplicate.**

Using keyboard shortcuts and hotkeys is an essential skill for people who work with computers. If you're interested in programming, try to use keyboard shortcuts whenever possible!

(You can quickly duplicate this menu item by pressing Ctrl+D in Windows or ⌘-D on a Mac.)

3 **Add some placeholder text, such as Menu Item.**

> Logo   Menu Item   Menu Item   Menu Item

That should do it for the header area.

ADD YOUR MAIN CONTENT

After you place your logo and navigation menu, you can add your body:

1 Create some lines that represent your main content.

To create lines, click the Line tool and choose Line.

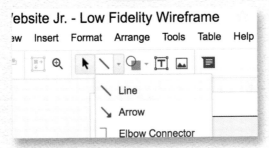

2 In the body section, create a line by clicking and dragging your mouse from left to right.

Leave enough room on the right side of the screen for your sidebar.

3 Add three more lines below the line you created in Step 2.

4 After you have four lines, draw several more lines that aren't quite as long as the four above them.

You can place a nice photograph in that area. (I tell you how later.)

Dino Image

5 Draw a rectangle for the image you want to use.

6 Continue drawing lines beneath the image.

CREATE A SIDEBAR AND SIDEBAR WIDGETS

You can also add a sidebar and a few sidebar widgets to your wireframe:

1 Draw a rectangle and place it to the right of the body content.

This will be your first widget.

2 Add some text, such as Featured Dinosaur.

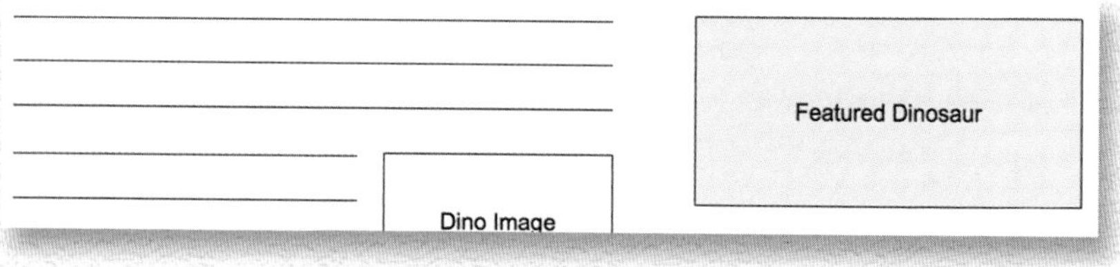

Featured Dinosaur

Dino Image

3 Duplicate this widget and place the second widget directly underneath the first one.

4 Add some text to your second widget.

Perhaps this time you create a Dinosaur Facts widget.

5 Duplicate the second rectangle, place it under the second rectangle, and name it.

CREATE A FOOTER

After you have all your widgets in place, you can add the final section, the footer:

1 Draw a long and wide rectangle to cover the bottom of the screen.

2 Add the word **Footer** to the rectangle.

YOUR FINISHED WIREFRAME

Great! You've assembled all the pieces of your first wireframe. You should have something that matches the very first figure in this project.

PROJECT 4 CREATE A STYLE GUIDE

IF YOU COMPLETED PROJECT 3 IN THIS BOOK, YOU CREATED A SIMPLE WIREFRAME SKETCH, WHICH CAN HELP YOU MAKE CHOICES FOR YOUR STYLE GUIDE. Creating a style guide can be a lot of fun because you pick colors and fonts (*fonts* are different styles of letters) to use on your web site pages. This project also goes over many different elements such as colors, typography, icons, and images and videos. Make sure to have your wireframe handy!

WHAT IS A STYLE GUIDE?

Think of a style guide as an instruction manual for you and others to follow when you create your web site.

For example, a style guide can include a logo, along with instructions about how someone can or cannot use that logo. It can also include a list of colors and maybe fonts that are okay to use with that logo. Style guides help you make your web site pages look like they belong together.

CREATE A STYLE GUIDE WITH FRONTIFY

You use a site map to plan the layout of your web site. Likewise, a style guide acts as a road map for your web site's look and feel. For this project, you create a basic style guide using a free service called Frontify. To use Frontify, you need to set up an account.

CREATE AN ACCOUNT WITH FRONTIFY

1 **Open a web browser.**

2 **In the address bar, type** https://frontify.com/ **and press Enter.**

3 **Near the top right of the page, you should see a button that reads Sign Up.**

4 Click the Sign Up button.

You should see a Sign-Up form in the middle of your screen.

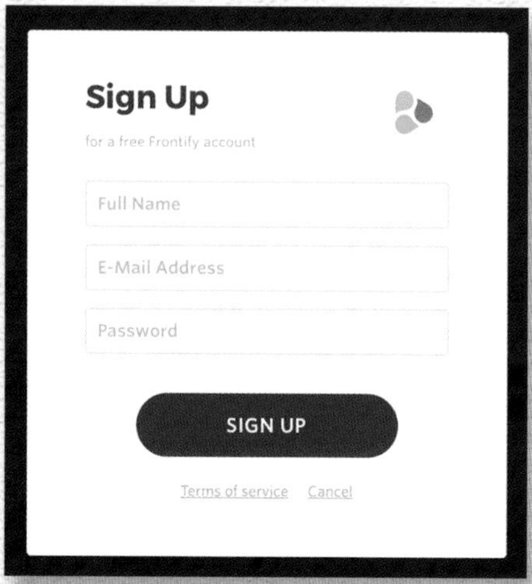

Sign Up

for a free Frontify account

Full Name

E-Mail Address

Password

SIGN UP

Terms of service   Cancel

5 With an adult's permission, type your name, email address, and a password.

6 Click the Sign Up button to continue.

Great job! You have created an account and are ready to create your very first style guide.

Sometimes when you sign up for Frontify, the web site asks you to fill out a survey. If a survey pops up, fill it out like this:

A few questions before we start...

Are you working on your own brand or for a customer?

Own Brand   Customer Brand

How big is the company behind the brand?

1-10   11-50   51-500   >500

How do you rate the maturity of the brand?

New   Young   Established   Global

Is there an existing style guide for the brand?

Yes   No

Continue

CREATE A BRAND WITH FRONTIFY

After you create an account in Frontify, the next step is to create your style guide. Frontify uses the word *brand* as its name for a style guide.

1 **Right after you register your account, you should see a small window that asks you to create a brand.**

2 **Type the name of your web site in the Brand or Company Name field.**

Create Brand

Brand or Company Name

Dinosaur Website

Brand Icon   Brand Color

Change Icon   #228CE0

Continue

3 Leave the Brand Icon as the house and the Brand Color as blue; you can change it later.

For this example, I enter Dinosaur Web site.

4 **Click Continue.**

A screen appears that asks whether you want to create a style guide from scratch or from a template. You can also set a title.

5 **Choose Template.**

6 **Select Basic Style Guide.**

WHAT'S A TEMPLATE?

A template is an empty guide to give you a head start on creating your style guide. You will see that when you choose to start with a template, the web site will guide you through first adding a logo, and then adding the basic colors. If you start with a blank style guide, you can add anything you want in any order. Sometimes it is helpful to use a template because then you don't have to remember everything and can instead just fill in the blanks!

7 On the same screen, click the Create Style Guide button.

Frontify takes you to your brand dashboard.

Don't worry about creating a logo at this point. You don't need a logo because you can use text in your web site header. To skip the logo, click Basics Colors at the bottom of the screen.

Next, you focus on learning about colors and fonts.

LEARN ABOUT COLOR CODES

As you know, people all over the world speak and write to each other in many different languages. You probably also know that computers use languages as well, although they're not the same as human languages. To create a web site, you will have to learn code (words from a computer language), and specifically *web color codes*.

HEX CODES

Web color codes can be written a lot of different ways; the most common way is using HEX codes. A HEX code can be a combination of letters and numbers with either three or six characters. Here are some examples of HEX codes and the color they stand for:

`#ff0000:`	Red
`#fff`	White
`#000`	Black
`#ffff00`	Yellow

Using a HEX code, you can create any one of more than 16 million colors! Cool, huh?

Thankfully, you don't need to remember all 16 million HEX codes because there is a tool that gives you the HEX code for the colors you want. The tool is called ColorHexa.

DISCOVER COLOR COMBINATIONS WITH COLORHEXA

Picking color schemes is a very important step in creating a web site. Color combinations affect how people feel about your site. Using tools like *ColorHexa* (http://www.colorhexa.com/) can make the process of building a color scheme very easy.

ColorHexa features an easy-to-use search bar, which allows you to enter the name of a color, such as yellow, to automatically receive a list of related colors right there in the search bar! This makes it very easy to choose a color.

ColorHexa is just one of dozens of web sites to help you work with colors. I also recommend visiting Adobe Color CC at https://color.adobe.com/ and Pantone Color Finder at http://www.pantone.com/ color-finder.

PICK THREE COLORS TO USE IN YOUR WEB SITE

Pick three colors to include in your style guide. You probably already have at least one color in mind. Maybe it's blue? Green? It's your choice.

1 **Open your web browser, type** http://colorhexa.com/**, and press the Enter key.**

2 **In the search bar, type the name of the first color you chose. This is called your Primary Color.**

3 **Click the first color listed in the drop-down list that appears.**

ColorHexa takes you to a page containing all the different codes for your Primary Color. The HEX code for your Primary Color appears at the very top of the screen, below the word *ColorHexa*.

Yellow / #ffff00 hex color

4 **Write down the HEX code on a piece of paper so that you can use it later. It's also a good idea to write down what your Primary Color is.**

yellow   ffff00

5 **Scroll down and you can see all the different ways that your Primary Color can be represented. In HEX code, yellow is ffff00, but in Binary code, yellow is represented as 11111111, 11111111, 00000000. HEX code is much easier to work with because it's so much shorter!**

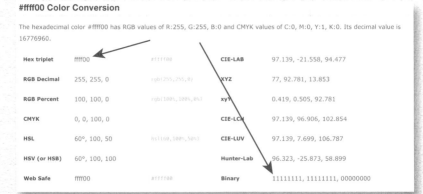

#ffff00 Color Conversion

The hexadecimal color #ffff00 has RGB values of R:255, G:255, B:0 and CMYK values of C:0, M:0, Y:1, K:0. Its decimal value is 16776960.

Hex triplet	ffff00	#ffff00	CIE-LAB	97.139, -21.558, 94.477
RGB Decimal	255, 255, 0	rgb(255,255,0)	XYZ	77, 92.781, 13.853
RGB Percent	100, 100, 0	rgb(100%,100%,0%)	xyY	0.419, 0.505, 92.781
CMYK	0, 0, 100, 0		CIE-LCH	97.139, 96.906, 102.854
HSL	60°, 100, 50	hsl(60,100%,50%)	CIE-LUV	97.139, 7.699, 106.787
HSV (or HSB)	60°, 100, 100		Hunter-Lab	96.323, -25.873, 58.899
Web Safe	ffff00	#ffff00	Binary	11111111, 11111111, 00000000

6 Keep scrolling down with the mouse until you see Color Schemes with (followed by your Primary Color's HEX code).

Color Schemes with #ffff00

Complementary Color   Analogous Color

7 Hover over the complementary color on the right with your mouse until you see a HEX code appear. This complementary color is called the Secondary Color.

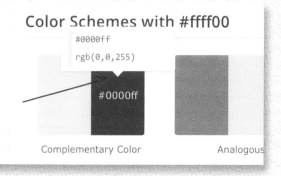

Color Schemes with #ffff00

#0000ff
rgb(0,0,255)

#0000ff

Complementary Color   Analogous

8 Write down the Secondary Color and its HEX code on your paper as well.

9 Move your mouse cursor and hover over the first Analogous Color to the left of your Primary Color. That color is called the Tertiary Color.

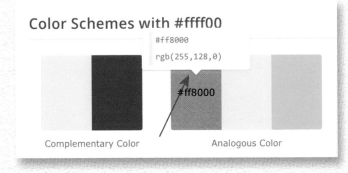

10 Write down the Tertiary Color and its HEX code on your paper.

Awesome! That was an important step toward creating a web site. Now you can put those colors into your style guide.

ADD A COLOR PALETTE TO FRONTIFY

By now, you have three colors for your web site and their HEX codes. You're ready to build a color palette in Frontify! A color palette is simply a place where you show a little bit of each color that will be in your web site.

1 Back in Frontify, you should see the Color page.

Colors

2 If you closed your Frontify browser tab, open your web browser, type https://frontify.com/, and press the Enter key.

3 Click the Login button near the top right.

4 You will see the Frontify brand dashboard. Click your brand tile.

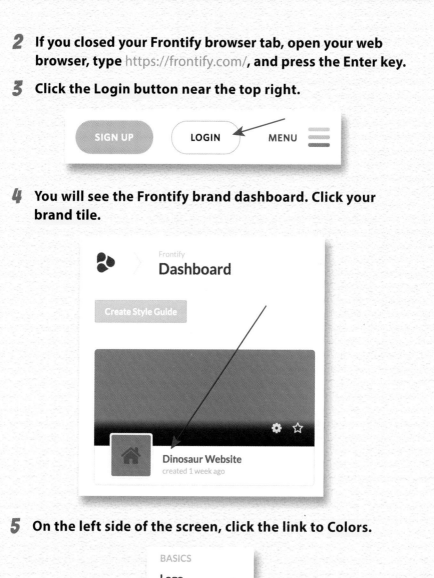

5 On the left side of the screen, click the link to Colors.

6 **In the top-right corner, click Edit, and you will see the page in Step 1.**

This turns on the Frontify editor, which lets you add the colors that you chose on ColorHexa and finish making your style guide.

7 **Scroll down with your mouse and look for the grayed-out section called New Color Palette, which has four grayed-out circles in it.**

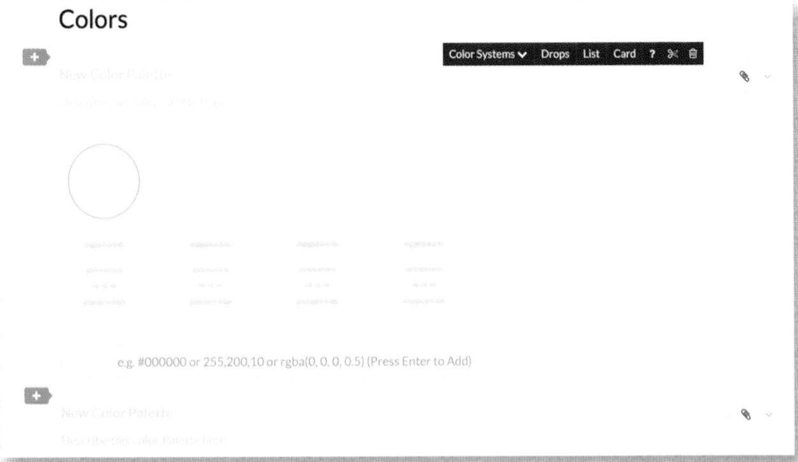

Colors

New Color Palette

Color Systems ✓   Drops   List   Card   ?   ✂   🗑

e.g. #000000 or 255,200,10 or rgba(0, 0, 0, 0.5) (Press Enter to Add)

New Color Palette

8 **Look for the input field underneath the four grayed-out circles, like the one shown with this step. It will have some example color HEX codes in it. This is where you**

enter the color HEX codes that you wrote down from ColorHexa. (If the input field isn't showing, go back up and click the Edit button again.)

e.g. #000000 or 255,200,10 or rgba(0, 0, 0, 0.5) (Press Enter to Add)

9 Type the color HEX code for your Primary Color into the input field.

ffff00

10 Press the Enter key to save your work, and you will see your Primary Color fill in the grayed-out circle above the input field.

Yellow

#FFFF00
255, 255, 0

Repeat Steps 8–10 for the other two colors you've chosen, your Secondary and Tertiary Colors. When finished, you will have three colors neatly arranged in your style guide!

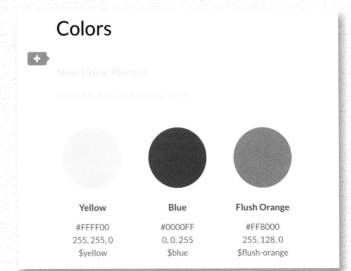

FIND A FONT WITH GOOGLE FONTS

Another Google tool that you are going to use to design your web site is Google Fonts.

Google Fonts is a free resource that allows users to choose and freely use different fonts on their web sites. Google Fonts has even taken the hard work out of font pairing. You can easily see a popular font combination and even see contrast between headlines and paragraph text.

Google Fonts isn't the only option for viewing free fonts. You can also look at the Open Font Library at https://fontlibrary.org/, or FontSquirrel https://fontsquirrel.com/.

The following process of finding fonts in Google Fonts can take a little time. Don't be afraid to look through a few different fonts.

1. **Open your web browser, type** https://fonts.google.com/, **and press Enter.**

2. **Scroll down. Look for an appealing font.**

   This step is up to you. You can choose any font you like! I choose Open Sans.

3. **After you have found a font you like, click the font's name in the upper-left corner of its area on the screen. You are taken to the font's information page, where you can see a specimen of that font — that is, what it looks like.**

   This figure shows two fonts: one for the heading and one for the paragraph. You can play around with choosing fonts that go well together! For this book, you concentrate on choosing one.

Open Sans	⊕
Roboto	Regular ▼
Open Sans	Regular ▼
Lato	⊕
Oswald	⊕
Raleway	⊕
Roboto Condensed	⊕

The spectacle before us was indeed sublime.

Apparently we had reached a great height in the atmosphere, for the sky was a dead black, and the stars had ceased to twinkle. By the same illusion which lifts the horizon of the sea to the level of the spectator on a hillside, the sable cloud beneath was dished out, and the car seemed to float in the middle of an immense dark sphere, whose upper half was strewn with silver. Looking down into the dark gulf below, I could see a ruddy light streaming through a rift in the clouds.

4 **Write down the name of the font you want to use on your web site.**

I've chosen Open Sans for my text (the one pictured in Step 3).

ADD YOUR FONT TO FRONTIFY

Now that you have a font picked out, you need to add the font to your style guide in Frontify.

1 **If you still have Frontify open on your Color Palette, click the button at the bottom of your screen that says Basic Typography and you should see a screen like the next figure.**

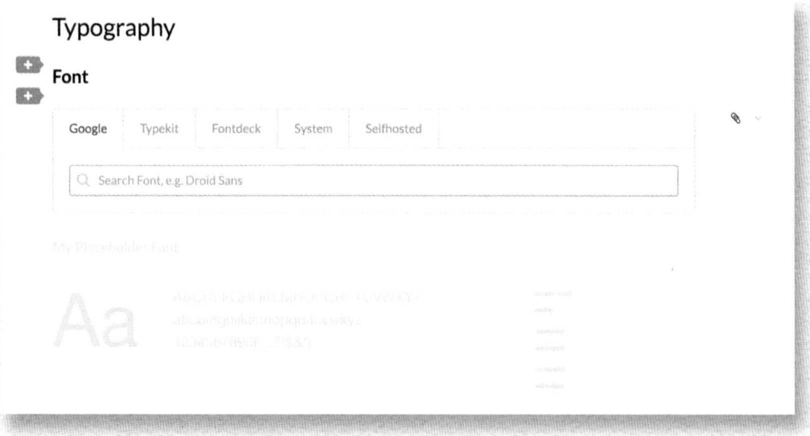

Typography

Font

| Google | Typekit | Fontdeck | System | Selfhosted |

Q Search Font, e.g. Droid Sans

My Placeholder Font

Aa

2 **If you have closed Frontify, open your web browser, type** https://frontify.com/**, and press the Enter key.**

3 **Click the Login button near the top right. Click your brand tile and then click the Edit button near the top as well.**

In the Frontify brand dashboard, on the left side of the screen, you should see a link called Typography.

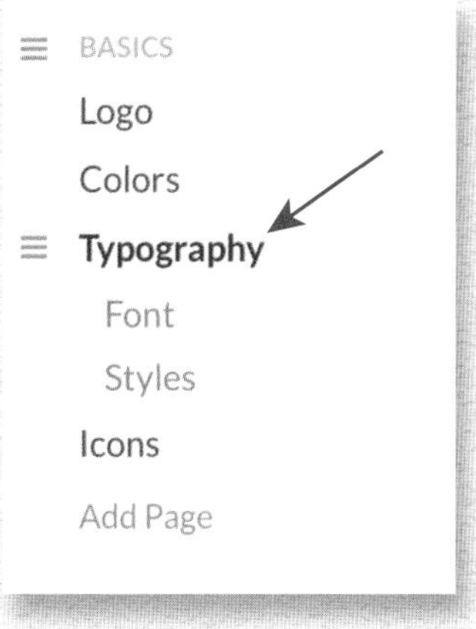

BASICS

Logo

Colors

≡ **Typography**

Font

Styles

Icons

Add Page

4 **Click Typography and you should see the screen in Step 1.**

5 **There is a search bar with different tabs, and the one that is already clicked is the Google tab. Type your font into the search bar and select the style you want from the list that appears.**

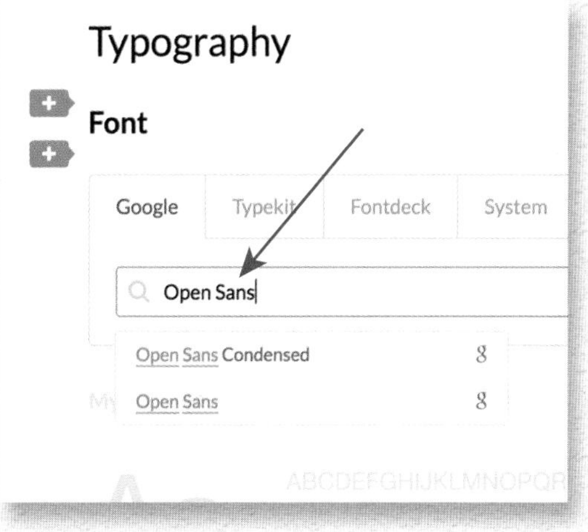

Typography

Font

| Google | Typekit | Fontdeck | System |

Open Sans

Open Sans **Condensed**   8

Open Sans   8

Awesome! You've successfully added your font to Frontify. If you scroll down, you should see your font in a few different styles, like *italics* and **bold**.

Just as the colors you chose in the previous section are in your style guide, now the font is part of your style guide as well. At the end of this project, when you're done with your style guide, you will use it as a guideline for *actually* making your web site!

FINDING AND USING MEDIA FROM THE WEB

Creating your own media can be fun, but sometimes drawing a lifelike image of a T-rex, well, it just doesn't make sense. Instead you could search for and use an image that someone else drew or photographed. This is a common practice and is referred to as using *stock photography*.

You have to follow some basic rules when you use someone else's images on your web site. The first rule is about the copyright (which I mention in this book's introduction). To use an image on your web site that you did not create, you need to make sure that the following is true: The media is licensed as public domain (CC0). *Public domain* means that the image is free for you to use, and you don't have to ask permission or say where the media came from. This is also called the Creative Commons license.

If you're not sure about licenses and what they mean, (it can be very confusing), you can read more about it at the Creative Commons (https://creativecommons. org/share-your-work/licensing-types-examples/).

My favorite web site for finding creative commons photos is VisualHunt (https://visualhunt.com). VisualHunt searches hundreds of stock photos for you, making it easy to get just the right photo.

USING VISUALHUNT TO FIND FREE STOCK PHOTOS

To finish up your style guide, you need to find a few images and place them into Frontify.

1 **Open your web browser, type** https://visualhunt.com/**, and press the Enter key.**

2 **Place your cursor in the search box and type what you are looking for.**

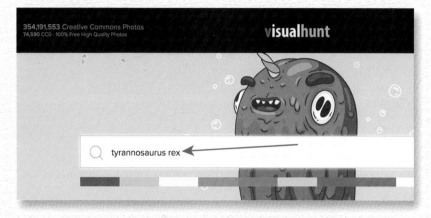

VisualHunt should return a few images.

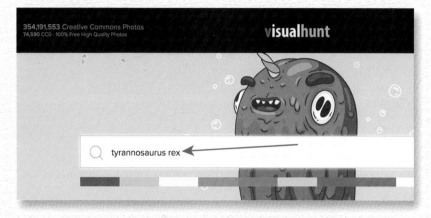

3 Just above the images, a License Type filter appears. Move your mouse cursor over Public Domain and click.

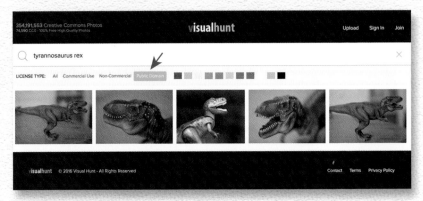

Notice how VisualHunt now displays only Public Domain images. These are free to use any way you want.

4 Click the image you want to add to your web site.

5 Move your mouse cursor to the right side of the web page. Click Download for Free.

6 Select the large size option (usually shown as L for large).

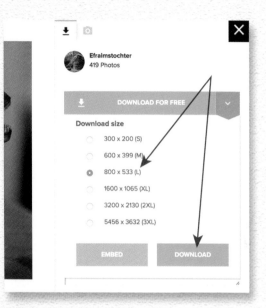

7 The file automatically saves to your computer when you click the big Download button.

ADD PHOTOS TO FRONTIFY

The previous section shows you how to get photos for your web site downloaded to your computer. In this section, you add them to Frontify. Getting them into Frontify is the last step in creating your style guide! Follow these steps:

1 If you don't already have Frontify open, type https:// frontify.com/ in your browser and press the Enter key.

2 Click the Login button at the top right. Then click the brand tile and then click the Edit button near the top right.

3 Move your mouse cursor to the left side of the screen and click Photography.

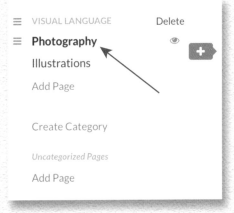

4 Move your mouse cursor to the middle of the screen. Click the image icon to open the upload dialog box.

5 Find your image on your computer, most likely in the Downloads folder (unless you decided to put it in a different folder). Double-click the filename of the image to upload it to Frontify.

Photography

6 Scroll down and move your mouse cursor over the image icon to upload another photograph. Repeat Steps 4 and 5 until you have uploaded all your images.

dino-dinosaur-tyrannosaurus-rex-replica-toys.jpg

Drop images here or click to upload

When you're finished, this page of your style guide should look something like the following figure.

dino-dinosaur-tyrannosaurus-rex-replica-toys.jpg

dino-dinosaur-tyrannosaurus-rex-replica-toys-3.jpg

dino-dinosaur-tyrannosaurus-rex-replica-toys-2.jpg

dino-dinosaur-tyrannosaurus-rex-replica-toys-4.png

Now you have your style guide! In the next project, you learn how to bring together your site map, wireframe, and style guide, combine a bit of coding, and make your very own web site.

YOU NOW HAVE A FULL DESIGN OF YOUR OWN WEB SITE. You have come up with a topic, made a site map to plan what pages you're going to have, made wireframes for your pages, and even created a style guide to help you with the look and feel of your site. Now it's time to add a bit of computer coding to actually make your web site!

In this project, you learn about HTML, a computer coding language that allows you to make a working web site. You will make all your pages, and even add images! In the next project, you get a chance to add a bit more color and interactivity to your web site.

SETTING UP YOUR CODING ENVIRONMENT

In Project 2, you used Google Drawings to make your site map. Now you will use Google Drive and some of the apps that connect to it to build and share your web site.

Before starting, you should have an adult's permission. (By law, you must be at least 13 years old to create any online account.)

CREATE YOUR GOOGLE FOLDER

First, you have to create a Google Folder.

1 **Open a web browser. The images in this book are using Chrome.**

2 In the address bar, type http://drive.google.com and press Enter. If you are signed in to Google, you should see something like what you see in the following figure.

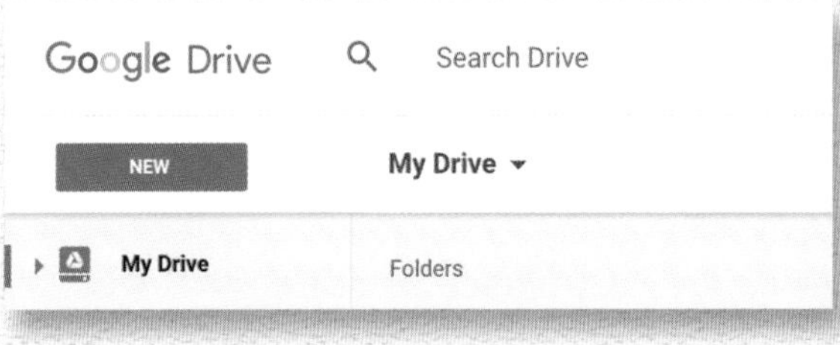

3 Create a new folder by clicking New and New Folder.

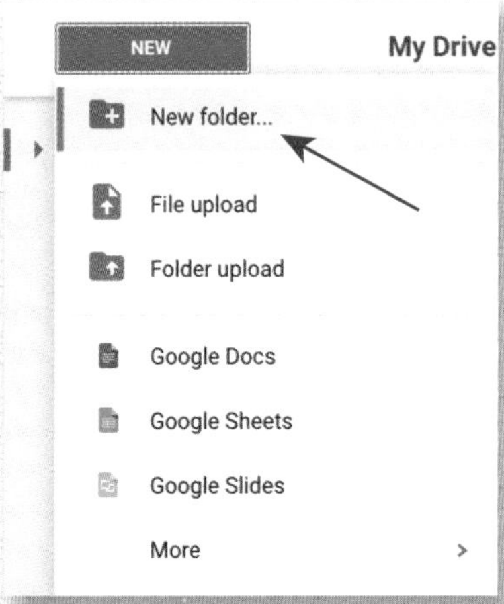

4 You can name your folder anything. In the following figure, the folder is called MyDinoSite.

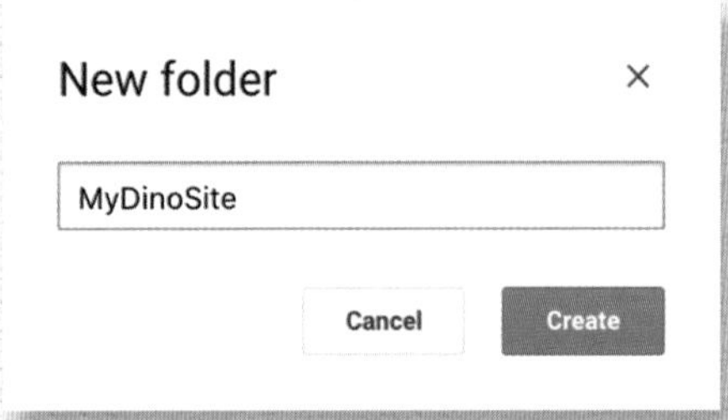

5 Double-click the new folder to open it.

This is where you will add all your coding files and image files for your web site.

ADD CODING APPS TO GOOGLE DRIVE

Now that you have your Google Folder, you can add a couple of apps that will make it easy for you to code your web site.

1 Click New, then More, then Connect More Apps.

2 A pop-up appears. Type HTML in the Search bar.

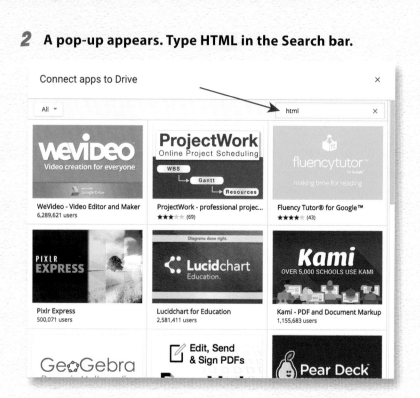

3 Press Enter, and you see an app called HTML Editey. Click the Connect button.

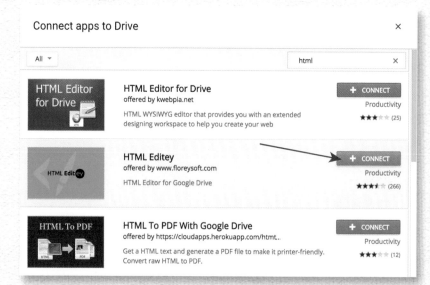

4 A pop-up will ask whether you want to make HTML Editey the default app for files it can open. This means every time you try to open a file with .html in the name, it will use HTML Editey to open the file. Click the box and then click OK.

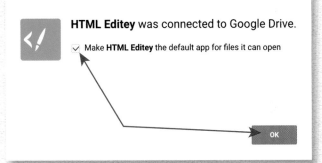

5 Scroll down in the pop-up from Step 3 until you find a second app called HTML Viewer. Click the Connect button.

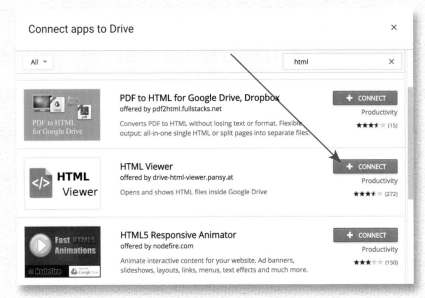

6 Just as in Step 4, a pop-up asks whether you want HTML Viewer to be the default app to open files that it can open. Click the box to take the check mark out this time, and click OK.

7 Close the pop-up and click New, then More. You should see HTML Editey there now. Click HTML Editey.

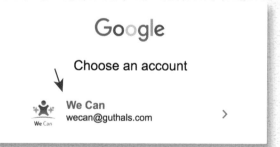

8 Google may ask you to choose an account to use this app with. If it does, choose the account you have been using.

9 **Google asks you to give Editey permission to use your account. Make sure you have an adult with you for this part, and then click Allow.**

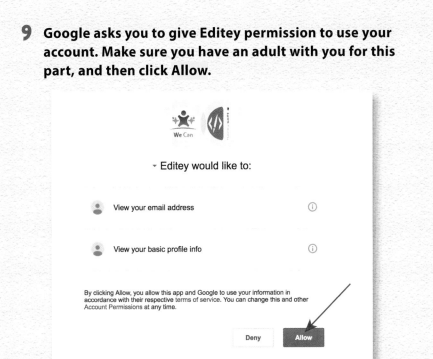

10 **Google may ask you again to choose an account to use this app with. If it does, choose the same account as you did in Step 8.**

11 Google will ask you *again* to give Editey permissions. With your adult's permission, click Allow.

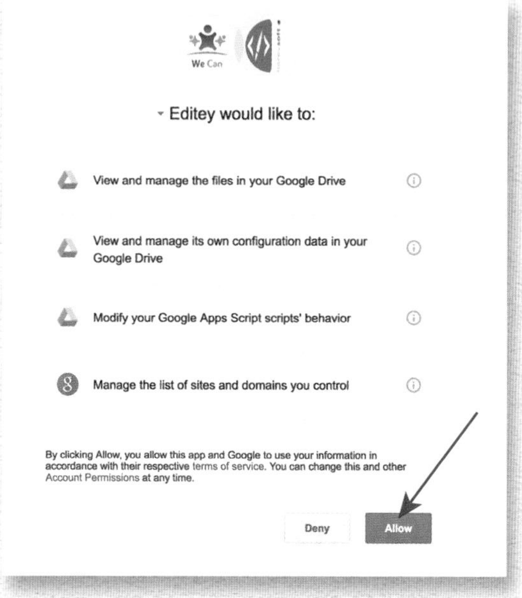

12 A pop-up appears with an introduction to Editey. Click Next after you have read through it.

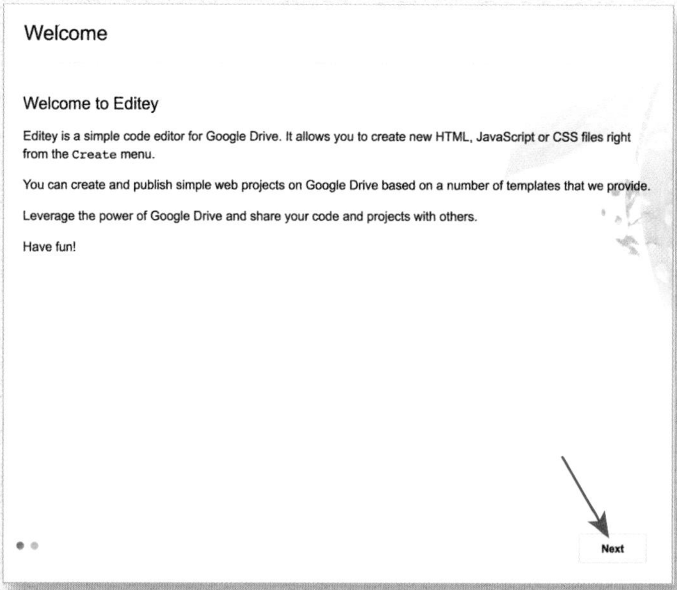

13 The next page of the pop-up is the agreement. Make sure you have an adult with you to read through this.

14 Scroll to the bottom of the pop-up and click both of the Agree boxes, and then click Done.

Welcome

COST OF PROCUREMENT OF SUBSTITUTE GOODS OR SERVICES, OR OTHER INTANGIBLE LOSS.

4.2. THE LIMITATIONS ON FLOREYSOFT'S LIABILITY TO YOU IN PARAGRAPH 4.1 ABOVE SHALL APPLY WHETHER OR NOT FLOREYSOFT HAS BEEN ADVISED OF OR SHOULD HAVE BEEN AWARE OF THE POSSIBILITY OF ANY SUCH LOSSES ARISING.

5. Other Content

5.1. The Services may include hyperlinks to other web sites or content or resources or email content. floreysoft may have no control over any web sites or resources which are provided by companies or persons other than floreysoft.

5.2. You acknowledge and agree that floreysoft is not responsible for the availability of any such external sites or resources, and does not endorse any advertising, products or other materials on or available from such web sites or resources.

5.3. You acknowledge and agree that floreysoft is not liable for any loss or damage which may be incurred by you or users of your Application as a result of the availability of those external sites or resources, or as a result of any reliance placed by you on the completeness, accuracy or existence of any advertising, products or other materials on, or available from, such web sites or resources.

☑ I agree to the Terms
☑ I agree to receive emails about product updates, downtime notifications, usability tips and about related product launches from floreysoft. Emails can be cancelled at any time by clicking on the unsubscribe link in the footer of the email.

Back   Done

15 At the top left of your screen, click where it says Untitled.html.

Untitled.html

File   Edit   View   Insert   Help

16 **Change the name to index.html and add a description if you want. Then click Rename.**

Rename file

Renaming this file will also change the filename on Google Drive

Enter a new file name:

index.html

Enter a description:

My Homepage.

Rename   Cancel

Congratulations! You are now ready to write your web site code.

NEW	My Drive > **MyDinoSite** ▾

▶ 📁 My Drive	Files
👥 Shared with me	
🕐 Recent	
🌀 Google Photos	
⭐ Starred	📄 Index.html
🗑 Trash	

CODING YOUR HOME PAGE

Wow, you have designed a web site and set up your coding environment. You are only a few steps away from becoming a real web site developer! This section teaches you a little bit about HTML, a coding language that is used for making web sites.

If you want to learn more HTML beyond this book, you should check out html://www.w3schools.com. Here you will find all kinds of HTML tutorials and even be able to test your coding.

THE HTML STRUCTURE

HTML is a coding language called a markup language. It's called a markup language because it is used to outline the page that you're making for a web site. When you're coding a web site, your code will always have the same basic structure.

```
HTML
   Head

   Body
      Header




      Footer
```

Not only do coding languages have certain structures, but each language also has a different *syntax*. You already know a bit about syntax, because in English you put a period at the end of a sentence and a question mark at the end of a question. The period and question mark is part of the syntax of English.

In HTML, there are a lot of greater-than and less-than signs in the syntax. But there is a pattern! Each section of an HTML file is surrounded by the name of the section in `<SectionName> </SectionName>`. We call the first part the open tag and the second one the close tag. Notice that the close tag has a / after the less-than symbol.

1 Go to your Internet browser again. You should still have index.html open in HTML Editey. If you don't, go to http://drive.google.com, double-click your project folder (like MyDinoSite), then right-click index.html and choose Open With HTML Editey.

2 Add the open tag for the HTML section, and you will notice that the close tag automatically gets added.

3 Looking back at the HTML structure at the beginning of this section, make sure that the tags you add here (shown in the figure) are inside the HTML tags.

```
Index.html
File   Edit   View   Insert   Help      All changes saved in Drive

  1   <html>
  2       <head>
  3
  4       </head>
  5       <body>
  6           <header>
  7
  8           </header>
  9
 10           <footer>
 11
 12           </footer>
 13       </body>
 14   </html>
 15
 16
 17
 18
 19
 20
 21
```

Awesome! You are now ready to start adding content to your HTML page! This project walks you through making the dinosaur example site, but everything you see here is an example of what you can do in your web site, too!

ADDING TEXT TO YOUR WEB SITE

Now that you have your web site structure ready, you can start adding text to display on it. Click between the close header tag and the open footer tag and type Hello World!.

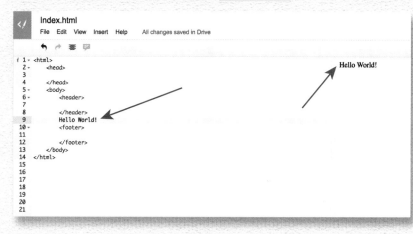

Notice that on the right side of your screen, the words "Hello World!" appear. That is because the right side of your screen is a preview of what your web site looks like.

In this section, you use your Project 3 final wireframe and code all the text.

Right now, you will just have placeholder text. That means that you won't write the actual text yet; you're just trying to make sure you know where everything will go.

ADDING MORE STRUCTURE TO YOUR WEB SITE

Adding text to your web site is good, but you might want to add a little more structure to your web site, too. For example, in the wireframe example from Project 3, there was a sidebar.

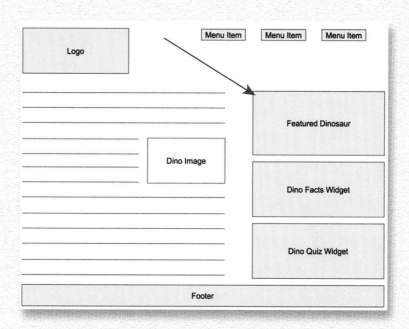

To add a different part of your web site, like a sidebar, you have to create new sections inside the body tags called "divs." The first div will go to the left and take up most of the screen, and the second div will go to the right and take up only a little of the screen. To create new divs, you use the open and close div tags: `<div>` `</div>`. Even if you do not want these divs to be next to each other, you might want to have different divs with different colors or content.

Look through your wireframe from Project 3 and put the text (or placeholder text) in the correct places. For example, in the web site in this book, the text about dinosaurs is on the left of the web site. The first div that was made in this example will be the one on the left, so that's why the dinosaur text is in the first div.

```
 1 <html>
 2     <head>
 3
 4     </head>
 5     <body>
 6         <header>
 7             Logo and Menu up here
 8         </header>
 9         <div>
10             Text about my Dinosaurs right here.
11         </div>
12         <div>
13
14         </div>
15         <footer>
16             Footer Down Here
17         </footer>
18     </body>
19 </html>
20
21
22
23
24
25
26
```

Logo and Menu up here
Text about my Dinosaurs right here.
Footer Down Here

ADD STYLE ATTRIBUTES TO YOUR WEB SITE

Next, you will add attributes to your div sections to change the color of them, making them easier to see them. Attributes can be a lot of different things in web sites. They can be colors, size, or even the font style!

Look carefully through the code and add the following bits (see the next figure).

You have to type everything in code exactly as it is in the book. If you capitalize something that shouldn't be capitalized, or add a space where there shouldn't be a space, your web site won't work. This is because computers, even though they are powerful, aren't that smart! So they don't know that the name Sarah is the same as sarah. To a computer, those two names are different because one has a capital S and the other has a lowercase s.

The head part of your web site is where you put your style code. You might want to refer to your style guide from Project 4 for this part. The example in this book uses orange, blue, and yellow for the colors and sans serif for the font, so that's what is shown here.

1   Between the head tags, add an open and close style tag.

```
i 1 ▾ <html>
  2 ▾     <head>
  3 ▾         <style>
  4 ▾             |
  5           </style>
  6       </head>
  7 ▾     <body>
  8 ▾         <header>
  9               Logo and Menu up here
 10           </header>
 11 ▾         <div>
 12               Text about my Dinosaurs right here.
 13           </div>
 14 ▾         <div>
 15
 16           </div>
 17 ▾         <footer>
 18               Footer Down Here
 19           </footer>
 20       </body>
 21   </html>
```

Logo and Menu up here
Text about my Dinosaurs right here.
Footer Down Here

2   Between the style tags, add a section called body. This section, instead of having the less-than and greater-than tags, will have open and close curly braces. Everything inside the body section will change what is in the body part in your code below.

```
i 1 ▾ <html>
  2 ▾     <head>
  3 ▾         <style>
  4 ▾             body {
  5
  6               }
  7           </style>
  8       </head>
  9 ▾     <body>
 10 ▾         <header>
 11               Logo and Menu up here
 12           </header>
 13 ▾         <div>
 14               Text about my Dinosaurs right here.
 15           </div>
 16 ▾         <div>
 17
 18           </div>
 19 ▾         <footer>
 20               Footer Down Here
 21           </footer>
 22       </body>
 23   </html>
```

Logo and Menu up here
Text about my Dinosaurs right here.
Footer Down Here

3   Add the following line exactly as it is written. When you finish typing it, your font will change!

```
i 1 ▾ <html>
  2 ▾     <head>
  3 ▾         <style>
  4 ▾             body {
  5                   font-family:'Open Sans', sans-serif;
  6               }
  7           </style>
  8       </head>
  9 ▾     <body>
 10 ▾         <header>
 11               Logo and Menu up here
 12           </header>
 13 ▾         <div>
 14               Text about my Dinosaurs right here.
 15           </div>
 16 ▾         <div>
 17
 18           </div>
 19 ▾         <footer>
 20               Footer Down Here
 21           </footer>
 22       </body>
 23   </html>
```

Logo and Menu up here
Text about my Dinosaurs right here.
Footer Down Here

4 Add the following line exactly as it is written. When you finish typing it, your web site should change to orange!

```
 i 1 ▾ <html>
   2 ▾   <head>
   3 ▾     <style>
   4 ▾       body {
   5             font-family:'Open Sans', sans-serif;
   6             background-color: #ff8000;
   7           }
   8         </style>
   9       </head>
  10 ▾   <body>
  11 ▾     <header>
  12           Logo and Menu up here
  13         </header>
  14 ▾     <div>
  15           Text about my Dinosaurs right here.
  16         </div>
  17 ▾     <div>
  18
  19         </div>
  20 ▾     <footer>
  21           Footer Down Here
  22         </footer>
  23       </body>
  24     </html>
```

Logo and Menu up here
Text about my Dinosaurs right here.
Footer Down Here

5 Change your style to the colors and fonts that you chose and watch your web site start to come to life.

6 Incredible! You are already making such good progress. Next, make sure you understand where your other sections are. Turn the header and footer into your secondary color from your style guide. In this book, the secondary color is blue.

```
 i 1 ▾ <html>
   2 ▾   <head>
   3 ▾     <style>
   4 ▾       body {
   5             font-family:'Open Sans', sans-serif;
   6             background-color: #ff8000;
   7           }
   8 ▾       header {
   9             background-color: #0000ff;
  10           }
  11 ▾       footer {
  12             background-color: #0000ff;
  13           }
  14         </style>
  15       </head>
  16 ▾   <body>
  17 ▾     <header>
  18           Logo and Menu up here
  19         </header>
  20 ▾     <div>
  21           Text about my Dinosaurs right here.
  22         </div>
  23 ▾     <div>
  24
  25         </div>
  26 ▾     <footer>
  27           Footer Down Here
  28         </footer>
  29       </body>
  30     </html>
```

Logo and Menu up here
Text about my Dinosaurs right here.
Footer Down Here

7 Next, you are going to turn your div sections into your tertiary color. In this book, the tertiary color is yellow.

```
1 ▾ <html>
2 ▾   <head>
3 ▾     <style>
4 ▾       body {
5             font-family:'Open Sans', sans-serif;
6             background-color: #ff8000;
7           }
8 ▾       header {
9             background-color: #0000ff;
10          }
11 ▾      footer {
12            background-color: #0000ff;
13          }
14 ▾      div {
15            background-color: #ffff00;
16          }
17        </style>
18      </head>
19 ▾    <body>
20 ▾      <header>
21          Logo and Menu up here
22        </header>
23 ▾      <div>
24          Text about my Dinosaurs right here.
25        </div>
26 ▾      <div>
27
28        </div>
29 ▾      <footer>
30          Footer Down Here
31        </footer>
32      </body>
33    </html>
```

Logo and Menu up here
Text about my Dinosaurs right here.
Footer Down Here

8 It would be more useful if you could see which div was where. To make the div sections have different-colored backgrounds, you can assign them to classes. An HTML style class is just a way of saying that everything in that class has the same style.

```
1 ▾ <html>
2 ▾   <head>
3 ▾     <style>
4 ▾       body {
5             font-family:'Open Sans', sans-serif;
6             background-color: #ff8000;
7           }
8 ▾       header {
9             background-color: #0000ff;
10          }
11 ▾      footer {
12            background-color: #0000ff;
13          }
14 ▾      div {
15            background-color: #ffff00;
16          }
17 ▾      .left {
18            background-color: #ffffff;
19          }
20 ▾      .right {
21            background-color: #000000;
22          }
23        </style>
24      </head>
25 ▾    <body>
26 ▾      <header>
27          Logo and Menu up here
28        </header>
29 ▾      <div class="left">
30          Text about my Dinosaurs right here.
31        </div>
32 ▾      <div class="right">
33
34        </div>
35 ▾      <footer>
36          Footer Down Here
37        </footer>
38      </body>
39    </html>
```

Logo and Menu up here
Text about my Dinosaurs right here.
Footer Down Here

Notice that the class style definition starts with a period.

In this book, the two divs are meant to be side by side. But your divs don't have to be like that; they could be one on top of the other. For example, this book names the classes for the divs "left" and "right," but you could name yours "top" and "bottom."

You might notice that the left div, which has gave a background color of #ffffff (which is white) shows up, but the right div, which has gave a background color of #000000 (which is black), doesn't. That's because there is nothing in the right div!

9 **Add some text in the right div (or the div that you haven't filled in), and that second div will show up; in this example, it's the black div.**

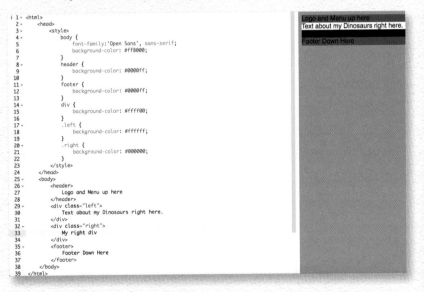

10 **Be careful! Sometimes you have your text and background colors the same, which makes it look like there is nothing there! In this book, the problem is that you can't see the text because the text and background are black. But never fear! There is a style attribute for text color, too.**

```
1 - <html>
2 -   <head>
3 -     <style>
4 -       body {
5           font-family:'Open Sans', sans-serif;
6           background-color: #ff8000;
7         }
8 -       header {
9           background-color: #0000ff;
10        }
11 -      footer {
12          background-color: #0000ff;
13        }
14 -      div {
15          background-color: #ffff00;
16        }
17 -      .left {
18          background-color: #ffffff;
19        }
20 -      .right {
21          background-color: #000000;
22          color: #ffffff;
23        }
24      </style>
25    </head>
```

The last problem is that the right div isn't actually on the right! It's underneath the left div. If you want to put two divs next to each other, you can use this formatting trick. To move a div to the right, you will have to add these style attributes:

» **Width:** The left div should be 75% width and the right div should be 25% width. That way, the left side takes up most of the screen, but the right side is still there.

» **Float:** This style attribute tells the div what it should do if there is room for it on the line before it. If there is room, it will push all the way to the left. This makes the right div go toward the left div.

Now that you know how to get two divs next to each other, you can play around with these style attributes! For example, you can have the left div be smaller than the right, or have them be equal. Use these to make the web site that *you* designed in the first four projects!

Keep adding divs, fonts, and colors until your web site looks like the wireframe that you made in Project 3.

Wow! Your web site is starting to come together. Even though it might look a little silly right now, you actually have your structure built and you have some colors down!

ADDING PICTURES TO YOUR WEB SITE

Now that you have everything in place, you can start adding a couple of pictures to your site.

1 **Go to http://drive.google.com and double-click your project folder. The one in this book is called MyDinoSite.**

2 **Click New and File Upload so that you can upload your first image to your Google Drive folder.**

3 Find your first picture on your computer. You might still have it saved in your Downloads folder. Then click Open. The one in this example is a dinosaur picture.

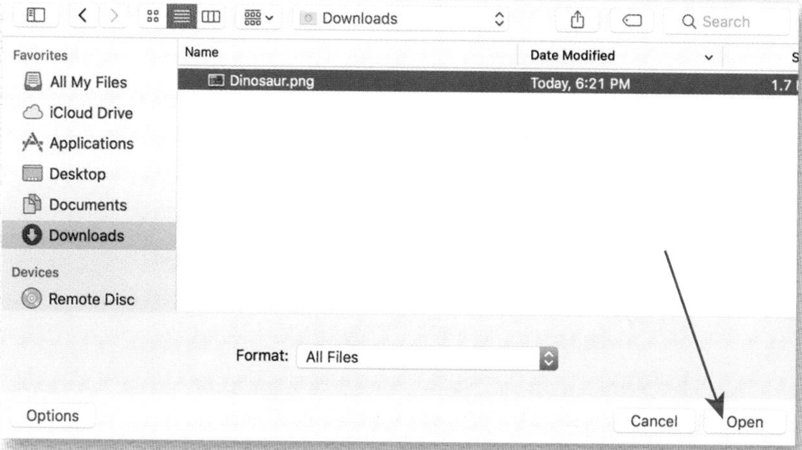

Favorites	Name	Date Modified	S
All My Files	Dinosaur.png	Today, 6:21 PM	1.7
iCloud Drive			
Applications			
Desktop			
Documents			
Downloads			
Devices			
Remote Disc			

Downloads

Q Search

Format: All Files

Options   Cancel   Open

4 On the bottom right of your screen, you should see the file uploading.

5 After it's done, you should see a green checkmark next to it. You should also see the image in your folder.

6 Right-click the image and then click Share.

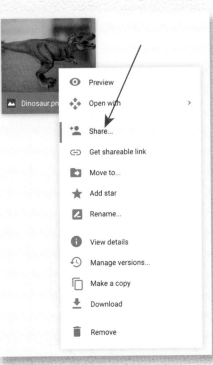

7 Click Advanced.

Share with others   Get shareable link 🔗

People

Enter names or email addresses...

Done ———————————————▶ Advanced

8 Click Change.

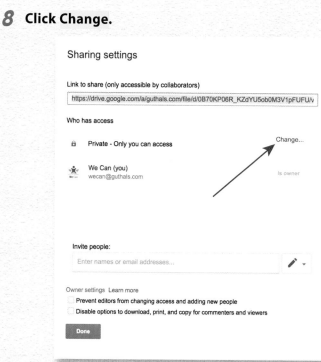

9 Choose On – Public on the Web and click Save.

10 Click Done.

Sharing settings

Link to share

ps://drive.google.com/file/d/0B70KP06R_KZdYU5ob0M3V1pFUFU/view?usp=sharing

Who has access

Public on the web - Anyone on the Internet can find and **view**   Change...

We Can (you)
wecan@guthals.com   Is owner

Invite people:

Enter names or email addresses...

Owner settings Learn more

☐ Prevent editors from changing access and adding new people
☐ Disable options to download, print, and copy for commenters and viewers

Done

11 Double-click your image, and it should open in large size on your screen.

12 Click the three dots on the top right and click Open in New Window.

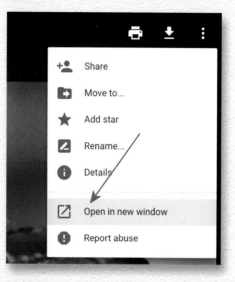

13 Click the three dots again and click Embed Item.

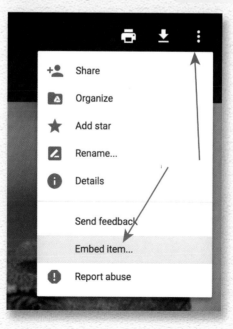

14 A pop-up shows you some HTML code. You know it's
HTML code because it has an open and close tag! Select
the HTML code by clicking where it is and pressing Ctrl+A
if you're on a Windows machine or ⌘-A if you're on a Mac.
Then copy the HTML code by pressing Ctrl+C if you are
on Windows or ⌘-C if you're on a Mac.

×

Embed item

Paste HTML to embed in website:

```
<iframe
src="https://drive.google.com/file/d/0B70KP06R_KZdYU5ob0M3V1pFUFU/preview"
width="640" height="480"></iframe>
```

OK

15 Go back to your HTML code for your web site and paste
the code between the header tags. To paste the code,
click next to the word Logo between your header tags
and press Ctrl+V if you're on Windows or ⌘-V if you're on
a Mac.

```
30 ▾    <body>
31 ▾        <header>
32              <iframe src="https://drive.google.com/file/d/0B70KP06R_KZdYU5ob0M3V1pFUFU/preview" width
                    ="640" height="480"></iframe>|
33              Logo and Menu up here
34          </header>
```

16 Because the image might be really big (as the dinosaur
one is in this example), you can change the width and
height of it. Try changing the width to 200 and the height
to 140.

```
<header>
    <iframe src="https://drive.google.com/file/d/0B70KP06R_KZdSDVrZGZ2QnVTQkk/preview"
        width="200" height="140"></iframe>
```

Congratulations! You have a picture in your code!

Even more exciting, you have a home page! In the next project, you will make the home page look exactly as you want it to. But before you do that, you need to create your other pages.

ADDING MORE PAGES TO YOUR WEB SITE

Now that you have a basic home page, you can add the other pages that you planned in your site map in Project 2. The site map example in this book has three new pages: types of dinosaurs, names of dinosaurs, and the dinosaur timeline.

1 **Go back to** http://drive.google.com **and double-click your project folder.**

2 **Right-click index.html and click Make a Copy.**

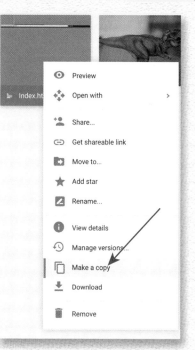

3 **Right-click the copy of index.html and click Rename.**

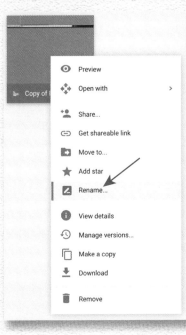

4 **Change the name to reference what you will put on that page. For example, for the page for types of dinosaurs in this book, the new HTML page is called** types.html. **Click OK.**

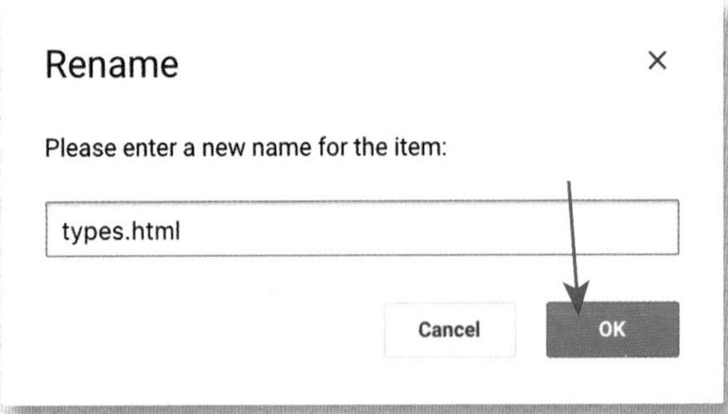

Rename   ×

Please enter a new name for the item:

types.html

Cancel   OK

5 Do this again until you make all of the pages you need. This example needs two more pages: names.html and timeline.html.

6 Highlight all the HTML files and images by clicking above and to the left of index.html and dragging your mouse over all of them.

7 Right-click index.html and click Share.

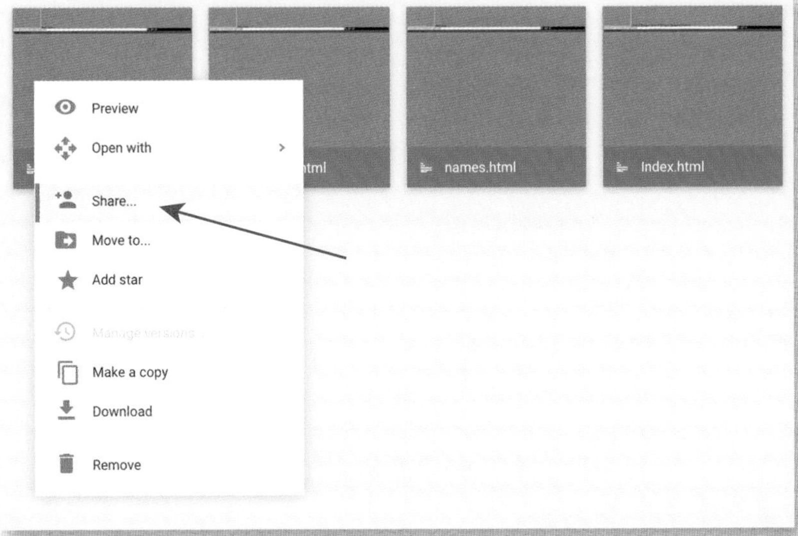
Preview
Open with
Share...
Move to...
Add star
Manage versions...
Make a copy
Download
Remove
names.html
Index.html

8 Just as you did for your first image, click Advanced. Then click Change and change it to be Public on the Web.

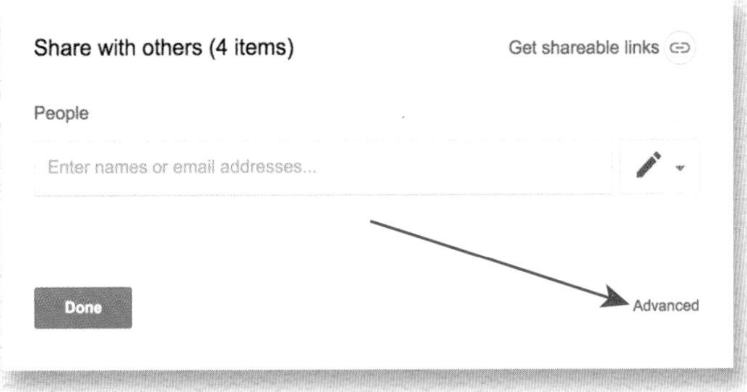
Share with others (4 items)
Get shareable links
People
Enter names or email addresses...
Done
Advanced

9 When you click Save, you should see that four files are all public. Click Done.

Sharing settings (4 items)

Links to share (4 links accessible):

usp=sharing
https://drive.google.com/file/d/0B70KP06R_KZdN0R5cUpubnNETUE/view?
usp=sharing

Who has access

🌐 Public on the web - Anyone on the Internet   Change...
can find and **view**

👤 We Can (you)   Is owner
wecan@guthals.com

Invite people:

Enter names or email addresses...   ✏️ ▾

Owner settings Learn more
☐ Prevent editors from changing access and adding new people
☐ Disable options to download, print, and copy for commenters and viewers

Done

10 **Right-click one of your new pages, such as types.html, and click Open With and then HTML Viewer.**

👁 Preview

➕ Open with   >   ⚠️ HTML Viewer

👤 Share...   📄 Google Docs

🔗 Get shareable link   ▣ HTML Editey

📥 Move to...   Suggested apps

⭐ Add star   📗 Drive Notepad

✏️ Rename...   + Connect more apps

ℹ️ View details

🔄 Manage versions...

📋 Make a copy

⬇️ Download

🗑 Remove

11 You should see the same thing as the home page (index. html), because you haven't changed what the new page looks like — you just copied the home page. That's okay for now.

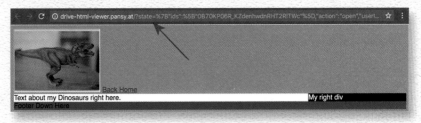

12 From the address bar, copy the URL by clicking it, highlighting it, and pressing Ctrl+C on Windows or ⌘-C on Mac.

13 Go back to your index.html file. If you closed it, you can re-open it by right-clicking index.html and clicking Open With and then HTML Editey.

14 Find your header and type in the HTML code for a link: <a href=YOUR_URL_HERE> </a>. (**Don't type the period.**)

```
31 ▾        <header>
32              <iframe src="https://drive.google.com/file/d/0B70KP06R_KZdSDVrZGZ2QnVTQkk
                    /preview" width="200" height="140"></iframe>
33              <a href="YOUR_URL_HERE">Types of Dinosaurs</a>|
34          </header>
```

15 Replace YOUR_URL_HERE with the URL you copied in Step 12. Do this by pressing Ctrl+V on Windows or ⌘-V on Mac.

```
31 ▾        <header>
32              <iframe src="https://drive.google.com/file/d/0B70KP06R_KZdSDVrZGZ2QnVTQkk
                    /preview" width="200" height="140"></iframe>
33              <a href="http://drive-html-viewer.pansy.at/?state=%7B%22ids%22
                    :%5B%220B70KP06R_KZdenhwdnRHT2RlTWc%22%5D,%22action%22:%22open%22
                    ,%22userId%22:%2211463255978908360521%22%7D">Types of Dinosaurs</a>
34          </header>
```

This is how you will link all your pages. You should make a link to all of your pages from your home page, just as you made a link to the first new page you added.

16 **Change the header background color to orange so that you can see the links.**

```
header {
    background-color: #ff8000;
}
```

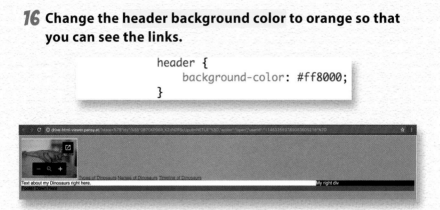

17 **Add a link back to the home page on each of your three other pages. You do this the same way you added a link to each page.**

 Make sure that you change the header color to orange for those pages, too! Otherwise it's really hard to see the links.

You can check out a working version by going to http://thewecan.zone/website-building and clicking MyDinoSite Project 5.

 Sometimes when you open your web site from a new browser window, it asks you to authorize it again. Just click Authorize.

You need to authorize the HTML Viewer to be able to view files. It will also be installed to your drive.

Authorize

Choose your account and click Allow.

Congratulations! You now have a working web site that goes to other pages! In the next project, you will learn how to make this web site match your wireframe and style guide.

PROJECT 6 MAKE YOUR WEB SITE LOOK GREAT

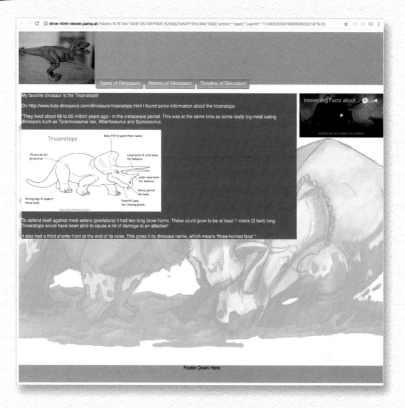

IF YOU HAVE BEEN FOLLOWING EACH PROJECT IN THIS BOOK, YOU ALREADY HAVE A WORKING WEB SITE THAT IS READY FOR YOU TO SHARE WITH THE WORLD. But some of the pieces are still missing. You made a site map, a wireframe, a style guide, and a basic web site.

But your web site doesn't have everything in each of your designs. The content in your site map isn't on the subpages; all your pages look like your homepage. The buttons, pictures, and content from your wireframe isn't on your home page, and the colors are kind of there, but they aren't in the right places.

This project will help you get your web site ready for all your friends and family to learn about the topic you chose. The example topic for this book is dinosaurs. You're going to put in all your content, add videos, and fix the colors so that your web site is inviting and fun!

GETTING GOOGLE DRIVE READY

Before you finish your web site, you need to get a few more things ready in your coding environment. For this project, your coding environment is Google Drive. You need to make your folder public, and you need to add another app to edit a style file (see the next section).

MAKE YOUR GOOGLE DRIVE FOLDER PUBLIC

Because you will be adding new files to your Google Drive folder, it is a good idea to make the entire folder public so that you can share your entire web site.

By making this folder public, everyone in the world can see what is inside. It is very important that you do not put any personal information in this folder. Make sure that you show an adult everything you plan to put on the Internet and that you ask permission to do that.

1 **Go to** http://drive.google.com **and log in to your Google account.**

2 **Right-click your project folder and click Share.**

3 Click advance and then Change. Choose Public on the Web and click Save. Now your entire folder should be public.

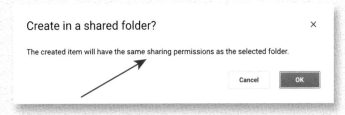

Now, any time you add a new file into this folder, Google will tell you that it will be public. Just click OK.

ADD THE CSS EDITEY APP TO GOOGLE DRIVE

As you might have noticed in the previous project, it can be really frustrating to have to copy and paste code that you write for your home page into each of your other pages. So instead of doing that, you will move all your style code to a new file. Then you will reference that file from your HTML code. The next section explains this more.

For now, add the CSS Editey app to Google Drive.

1 **Go to http://drive.google.com and log in to your Google account if you're not logged in already.**

2 **Double-click your project folder to open it.**

3 **Click New, then More, then Connect More Apps.**

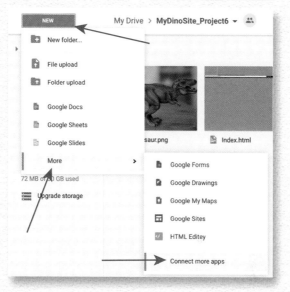

4 **Search "CSS" and click Enter. Click Connect next to CSS Editey.**

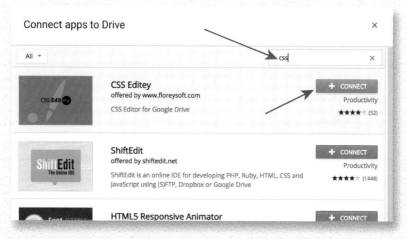

5 Click OK when Google asks if it should open CSS files with CSS Editey.

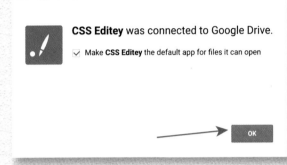

Now your coding environment is ready!

CREATING A CSS FILE FOR STYLE

In this section, you will move all your style code from your HTML files into one CSS file. CSS is another programming language, and it stands for **C**ascading **S**tyle **S**heet. You have already written CSS code without even realizing it! All the code inside the `head` section of your HTML file between the style tags is the CSS code.

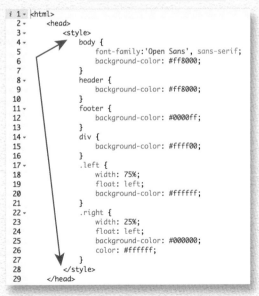

```
 1 ▾ <html>
 2 ▾   <head>
 3 ▾     <style>
 4 ▾       body {
 5             font-family:'Open Sans', sans-serif;
 6             background-color: #ff8000;
 7           }
 8 ▾       header {
 9             background-color: #ff8000;
10           }
11 ▾       footer {
12             background-color: #0000ff;
13           }
14 ▾       div {
15             background-color: #ffff00;
16           }
17 ▾       .left {
18             width: 75%;
19             float: left;
20             background-color: #ffffff;
21           }
22 ▾       .right {
23             width: 25%;
24             float: left;
25             background-color: #000000;
26             color: #ffffff;
27           }
28         </style>
29     </head>
```

CREATE A CSS FILE

First, you need the file to move all your CSS code into.

1 **Go to** http://drive.google.com **and double-click your project folder to open it.**

2 **Click New, then More, then CSS Editey.**

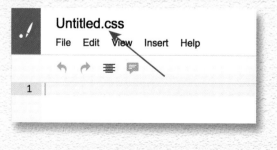

3 **Google might tell you that your file will have the same permissions as the folder. This means that your new file will be public, which is good. Click OK.**

4 **Click Untitled.css in the top left of your new file.**

5 **Change the name to style.css and click Rename.**

Rename file

Renaming this file will also change the filename on Google Drive

Enter a new file name:

style.css

Enter a description:

Rename   Cancel

MOVE YOUR STYLE CODE TO YOUR CSS FILE

Now it's time to move your style code from your HTML file to your CSS file.

1 **Go to** http://drive.google.com **and double-click your project folder to open it.**

2 **Right-click your index.html file. Then go to Open With and click HTML Editey.**

3 Highlight the code between your style tags and press Ctrl+C if you're on Windows or ⌘-C if you're on Mac to copy the code.

```
i 1 ▾ <html>
  2 ▾    <head>
  3 ▾       <style>
  4 ▾          body {
  5                 font-family:'Open Sans', sans-serif;
  6                 background-color: #ff8000;
  7             }
  8 ▾          header {
  9                 background-color: #ff8000;
 10             }
 11 ▾          footer {
 12                 background-color: #0000ff;
 13             }
 14 ▾          div {
 15                 background-color: #ffff00;
 16             }
 17 ▾          .left {
 18                 width: 75%;
 19                 float: left;
 20                 background-color: #ffffff;
 21             }
 22 ▾          .right {
 23                 width: 25%;
 24                 float: left;
 25                 background-color: #000000;
 26                 color: #ffffff;
 27             }
 28       </style>
 29    </head>
```

4 Open your style.css file and click into the file editor. Click Ctrl+V if you're on Windows and ⌘-V if you're on Mac to paste in your style code.

```
style.css
File   Edit   View   Insert   Help        All changes saved in Drive

  1 ▾          body {
  2                 font-family:'Open Sans', sans-serif;
  3                 background-color: #ff8000;
  4             }
  5 ▾          header {
  6                 background-color: #ff8000;
  7             }
  8 ▾          footer {
  9                 background-color: #0000ff;
 10             }
 11 ▾          div {
 12                 background-color: #ffff00;
 13             }
 14 ▾          .left {
 15                 width: 75%;
 16                 float: left;
 17                 background-color: #ffffff;
 18             }
 19 ▾          .right {
 20                 width: 25%;
 21                 float: left;
 22                 background-color: #000000;
 23                 color: #ffffff;
 24             }
```

The way your code is written in your file really matters because it helps you understand what code is where. HTML and CSS Editey make this easy! Just click the Format Source Code button and your code will move so that it is easier to read!

LINK YOUR CSS FILE TO YOUR HTML FILE

Now that your style code is in its own file, you need to tell your HTML file where it can find the style code.

This is going to be a little strange. You have to get the URL exactly right for it to work properly, so do this part slowly and ask an adult for help if you need it.

1 Open your index.html file and write the code to link your CSS file between the two <head> </head> tags.

```
<link rel="stylesheet" type="text/css" href=
    http://editey.com/preview/ID_NUMBER/style.css>
```

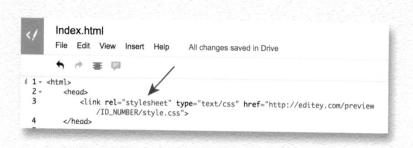

Everything you type should be exactly as it is in the code just above this paragraph. Don't add any spaces and don't get rid of any, and make sure everything is capitalized the same. This code is supposed to be all on one line, but as you see in the figure, depending on how wide your window is, the line of code can be split. That's okay! Just make sure that when you type it in, you never press Enter — you just type it in all at one time.

2 **You need to replace ID_NUMBER with the actual ID number of your style.css file. Open your style.css file and look at the URL from the address bar. The format is css.editey.com/file/ID_NUMBER/FILE_NUMBER.**

```
← → C  ⓘ css.editey.com/file/0B7OKPO6R_KZdUHdQTVROMzFrWWs/0B7OKPO6R_KZdb3djeFd0V2c5Y3c#
```
style.css
File Edit View Insert Help   All changes saved in Drive

```
1 ▾ body {
2      font-family:'Open Sans', sans-serif;
```

3 **Highlight the ID_NUMBER and press Ctrl+C if you're on Windows, ⌘-C if you're on Mac, to copy it.**

```
← → C  ⓘ css.editey.com/file/0B7OKPO6R_KZdUHdQTVROMzFrWWs/0B7OKPO6R_KZdb3djeFd0V2c5Y3c#
```
style.css
File Edit View Insert Help   All changes saved in Drive

```
1 ▾ body {
2      font-family:'Open Sans', sans-serif;
3      background-color: #ff8000;
4  }
5 ▾ header {
6      background-color: #ff8000;
```

4 **Open your index.html file and highlight the ID_NUMBER from Step 1.**

5 **Press Ctrl+V if you're on Windows, ⌘-V if you're on Mac, to paste the ID number in the URL.**

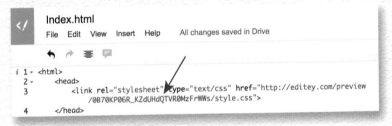

6 **Copy the entire `<link` line of code and paste it into the other three html files that you made in your previous project.**

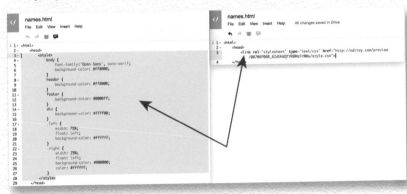

To open each HTML file, go to *http://drive.google.com*, open your project folder, right-click the file you want to open, and choose HTML Editey.

You should delete the style tags in all the HTML files. You need only the link tag now.

TEST YOUR CHANGES

Wow! You just made a lot of changes that could potentially hurt your web site. Before moving on, you should test to make sure everything still works.

1 Go to *http://drive.google.com* **and open your project folder.**

2 Right-click index.html, go to Open With, and click HTML Viewer.

3 If your style isn't showing up, click the Refresh button.

After all that work, your web site should look the same as it did at the end of the Project 5. Now you are ready to make changes to make it look better, and it will be much easier to make those changes!

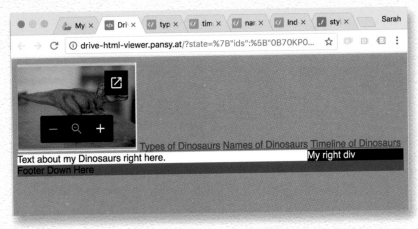

When you test your web site, make sure to click all the buttons on your web site to make sure they all still work. Just because something looks right doesn't mean it is acting right!

STYLING YOUR WEB SITE

Now that you have a style.css file, you can update the style of your web site quickly! Before you add more content, you should fix the style.

DECIDE WHERE TO PUT THE BACKGROUND COLORS

You can decide where to put the different colors yourself, but one way to help you decide is to look up other web sites with similar colors.

You should always ask an adult's permission before looking anything up on the Internet.

If you're following the example in this book using orange and blue, you might change your header and footer to be orange, your left and right class to be blue, and your body to be white. The background color attribute (the name of the color for your background) is `background-color`.

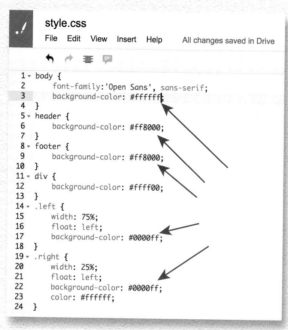

CHANGE THE FONT COLOR

Now that you have your background colors how you want them, change the text so that it's easy to read.

1 **You might have to play around with the different colors. For the example of using orange and blue, the text in the body looks best as white. The font color attribute (the name of the color for your text) is `color`.**

```
body {
    font-family:'Open Sans', sans-serif;
    background-color: #ffffff;
    color: #ffffff;
}
```

2 For an orange background, or other colors like orange, the white text doesn't look as good. If the white text doesn't look good on one of your colors, change the text to be a different color. For example, on an orange background, you would change the color of the text in your footer to be black (`color: #000000`).

FORMAT YOUR PAGE

You can do a few simple things to make your web site look even better! Follow these steps to format your page.

1 Center the text of the footer. To move the text to the left, right, or center, you use the text-align attribute. This is a good idea for any web site.

```
footer {
    background-color: #ff8000;
    color: #000000;
    text-align: center;
}
```

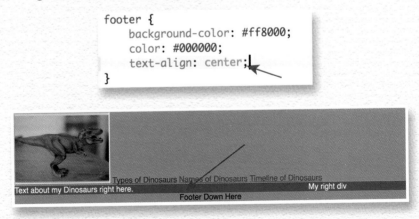

2 If you decided to have a sidebar on your site, such as the right class in this example, you might want to separate it from the left side. If you want divs to have space between them, you first reduce the width of one of the classes. Then add a margin attribute to put a margin next to it. Because this example shows the right class as the one highlighting interesting information, the width of the right class is reduced to 22% to leave room for the margin. Then the margin-left attribute is used to put a 10-pixel margin to the left of the right class.

```css
.right {
    width: 22%;  ◄──────────
    float: left;
    background-color: #0000ff;
    color: #ffffff;
    margin-left: 10px;  ◄──────
}
```

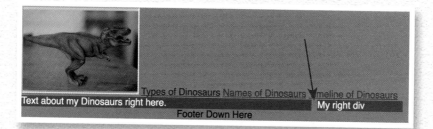

3 It is important to keep all your files up to date. You might have noticed that in this example, the div style definition isn't being used. It's okay to delete your extra style definitions if they are no longer needed. Just be careful that you do not delete one that you are using!

```css
14 ▾ div {
15      background-color: #ffff00;
16  }
```

4 Sometimes you want to make a style change to a lot of divs at one time. You can do this easily by wrapping one div around other ones. For example, back in index.html in this book, a new div is added around the left and right divs and named "content." That way, any style definition for "content" will affect both the left and right div!

```
Index.html
File   Edit   View   Insert   Help       All changes saved in Drive

1   <html>
2
3     <head>
4        <link rel="stylesheet" type="text/css" href="http://editey.com/preview
            /0B70KP06R_KZdUHdQTVR0MzFrWWs/style.css">
5     </head>
6
7     <body>
8        <header>
9           <iframe src="https://drive.google.com/file/d/0B70KP06R_KZdSDVrZGZ2QnVTQkk
               /preview" width="200" height="140"></iframe>
10          <a href="http://drive-html-viewer.pansy.at/?state=%7B%22ids%22
               :%5B%220B70KP06R_KZdenhwdnRHT2R1TWc%22%5D,%22action%22:%22open%22
               ,%22userId%22:%22114632559789083605218%22%7D">Types of Dinosaurs</a>
11          <a href="http://drive-html-viewer.pansy.at/?state=%7B%22ids%22
               :%5B%220B70KP06R_KZdRGM0dnItMXhUWU0%22%5D,%22action%22:%22open%22
               ,%22userId%22:%22114632559789083605218%22%7D">Names of Dinosaurs</a>
12          <a href="http://drive-html-viewer.pansy.at/?state=%7B%22ids%22
               :%5B%220B70KP06R_KZdeVV4MHBCNkU0STA%22%5D,%22action%22:%22open%22
               ,%22userId%22:%22114632559789083605218%22%7D">Timeline of Dinosaurs</a
               >
13       </header>
14       <div class="content">
15          <div class="left">Text about my Dinosaurs right here.
16          </div>
17          <div class="right">My right div
18          </div>
19       </div>
20       <footer>Footer Down Here
21       </footer>
22     </body>
23
24   </html>
```

5 In style.css, add a new style definition for any new classes that you create, like the content class.

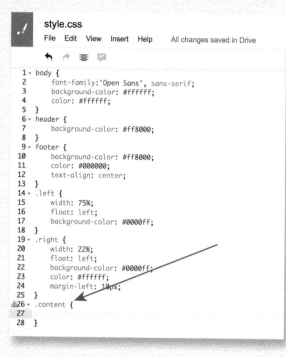

6 One trick to making sure your web site is always covering the entire screen and your footer is always at the bottom is to set the vertical height to your header, footer, and the main area (in this example, the content div). For this example, the height of the content style definition is 80%, the height of the header is 15%, and the height of the footer is 5%. This will make the header, footer, and content always fit on the screen, no matter what size the screen is.

```
style.css
File   Edit   View   Insert   Help       All changes saved in Drive

↩  ↪  ☰  💬

 1 ▾ body {
 2        font-family:'Open Sans', sans-serif;
 3        background-color: #ffffff;
 4        color: #ffffff;
 5   }
 6 ▾ header {
 7        background-color: #ff8000;
 8        height: 15%;
 9   }
10 ▾ footer {
11        background-color: #ff8000;
12        color: #000000;
13        text-align: center;
14        height: 5%;
15   }
16 ▾ .left {
17        width: 75%;
18        float: left;
19        background-color: #0000ff;
20   }
21 ▾ .right {
22        width: 22%;
23        float: left;
24        background-color: #0000ff;
25        color: #ffffff;
26        margin-left: 10px;
27   }
28 ▾ .content {
29        height: 80%;
30   }
```

7 After you have fixed the vertical sizing, try resizing your window to see the footer moving.

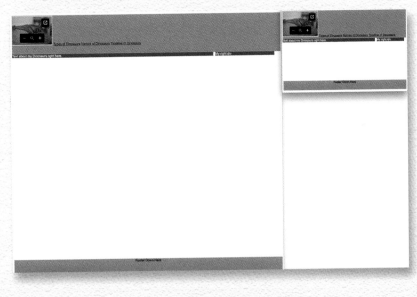

8 If you added the content div, to make sizing your web site easier, make sure you go to your other HTML files and add the content div around their divs also.

STYLIZE YOUR LINKS

The links on your web site just look like text. You can use CSS to make them look like nice buttons!

1 Go to https://css-tricks.com/examples/ButtonMaker/#.

2 Use the toggles and change the colors until you have a button that you like. Then click the button View the CSS.

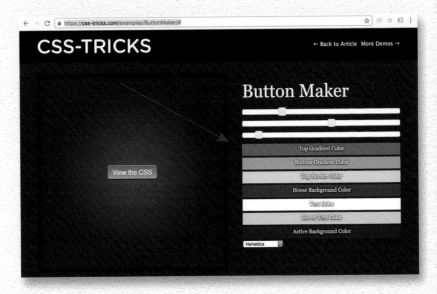

3 Highlight all the code and press Ctrl+C if you're on Windows and ⌘-C if you're on Mac to copy it.

```
The CSS                                                                      ✕

.button {
    border-top: 1px solid #96d1f8;
    background: #65a9d7;
    background: -webkit-gradient(linear, left top, left bottom, from(#3e779d), to(#65a9d7));
    background: -webkit-linear-gradient(top, #3e779d, #65a9d7);
    background: -moz-linear-gradient(top, #3e779d, #65a9d7);
    background: -ms-linear-gradient(top, #3e779d, #65a9d7);
    background: -o-linear-gradient(top, #3e779d, #65a9d7);
    padding: 6.5px 13px;
    -webkit-border-radius: 4px;
    -moz-border-radius: 4px;
    border-radius: 4px;
    -webkit-box-shadow: rgba(0,0,0,1) 0 1px 0;
    -moz-box-shadow: rgba(0,0,0,1) 0 1px 0;
    box-shadow: rgba(0,0,0,1) 0 1px 0;
    text-shadow: rgba(0,0,0,.4) 0 1px 0;
    color: white;
    font-size: 17px;
    font-family: Helvetica, Arial, Sans-Serif;
    text-decoration: none;
    vertical-align: middle;
    }
.button:hover {
    border-top-color: #28597a;
    background: #28597a;
    color: #ccc;
    }
.button:active {
    border-top-color: #1b435e;
    background: #1b435e;
    }
```

4 **Go to your style.css file and press Ctrl+V or ⌘-V to paste the code.**

```css
style.css
File   Edit   View   Insert   Help      All changes saved in Drive

1 ▾ body {
2        font-family:'Open Sans', sans-serif;
3        background-color: #ffffff;
4        color: #ffffff;
5   }
6 ▾ header {
7        background-color: #ff8000;
8        height: 15%;
9   }
10 ▾ footer {
11       background-color: #ff8000;
12       color: #000000;
13       text-align: center;
14       height: 5%;
15  }
16 ▾ .left {
17       width: 75%;
18       float: left;
19       background-color: #0000ff;
20  }
21 ▾ .right {
22       width: 22%;
23       float: left;
24       background-color: #0000ff;
25       color: #ffffff;
26       margin-left: 10px;
27  }
28 ▾ .content {
29       height: 80%;
30  }
31
32 ▾ .button {
33       border-top: 1px solid #96d1f8;
34       background: #65a9d7;
35       background: -webkit-gradient(linear, left top, left bottom, from(#3e779d), to(#65a9d7));
36       background: -webkit-linear-gradient(top, #3e779d, #65a9d7);
37       background: -moz-linear-gradient(top, #3e779d, #65a9d7);
38       background: -ms-linear-gradient(top, #3e779d, #65a9d7);
39       background: -o-linear-gradient(top, #3e779d, #65a9d7);
40       padding: 6.5px 13px;
41       -webkit-border-radius: 4px;
42       -moz-border-radius: 4px;
43       border-radius: 4px;
44       -webkit-box-shadow: rgba(0,0,0,1) 0 1px 0;
45       -moz-box-shadow: rgba(0,0,0,1) 0 1px 0;
46       box-shadow: rgba(0,0,0,1) 0 1px 0;
47       text-shadow: rgba(0,0,0,.4) 0 1px 0;
48       color: white;
49       font-size: 17px;
50       font-family: Helvetica, Arial, Sans-Serif;
51       text-decoration: none;
52       vertical-align: middle;
53       }
54 ▾ .button:hover {
55       border-top-color: #28597a;
56       background: #28597a;
57       color: #ccc;
58       }
59 ▾ .button:active {
60       border-top-color: #1b435e;
61       background: #1b435e;
62       }
```

5 **Go to index.html and add** `class="button"` **to each of your a tags.**

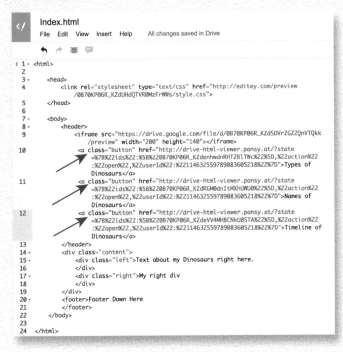

6 **Go to your other HTML files and add** `class="button"` **to the a tags.**

```
10          <a class="button" href="http://drive-html-viewer.pansy.at/?state
                =%7B%22ids%22:%5B%220B70KP06R_KZdN0R5cUpubnNETUE%22%5D,%22action%22
                :%22open%22,%22userId%22:%2211463255978908360521B%22%7D">Back Home</a>
```

CHANGE YOUR BACKGROUND

The background of your content area is just white. This section walks you through changing it to an image instead.

1 **Go to your style.css file and add** `background-image: url("IMAGE_URL");` **to your content style definition.**

```
29 ▼  .content {
30         height: 80%;
31         background-image: url("IMAGE_URL");
```

2 If you want to use a dinosaur picture, you can go to http://www.thewecan.zone/website-building and click Dino.png. Otherwise, just find your own background image by searching on google.com. Remember to always ask permission from a parent first!

3 Copy the URL of the image you found from the address bar. Highlight the URL and press Ctrl+C if you're on Windows and ⌘-C if you're on Mac. If you decided to find your own image, you can right-click the image and press Copy Image Address instead of copying the URL from the address bar.

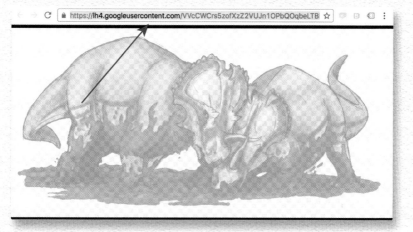

4 Paste the URL where it says IMAGE_URL from Step 1.

```
29 - .content {
30     height: 80%;
31     background-image: url("https://lh4.googleusercontent.com/vsHH2MeOrM1dyUbgZBfKaY1GyxrSI9zMwkfG6PQPGeNNmfGL1ZoGA1qDx7KST0TOmFePZ15voqPWSEk-m2754-h2438-rw");
```

5 Add two more lines of code to your content style definition. `background-size: cover;` will make sure that the image fills the entire content area, and `background-position: center;` will make sure that the image is centered on your page.

```
29 - .content {
30     height: 80%;
31     background-image: url("https://lh4.googleusercontent.com/vsHH2MeOrM1dyUbgZBfKaY1GyxrSI9zMwkfG6PQPGeNNmfGL1ZoGA1qDx7KST0TOmFePZ15voqPWSEk-m2754-h2438-rw");
32     background-size: cover;
33     background-position: center;
34 }
```

ADD YOUR CONTENT

Here comes the fun part! Add all your content about your topic into all your pages! If you had left and right divs, as in this example, add text about your dinosaurs on the left, and media on the right!

ADD CONTENT AND WIDGETS TO YOUR HOME PAGE

First, you can add some information about your favorite fact in your topic. In this example, it is about a triceratops. You can also add fun widgets, like YouTube videos, into your sidebar!

1 **Delete the placeholder text that says "Text about my topic right here" and write about your topic instead.**

```
<div class="left">My favorite dinosaur is the Triceratops!
    <br>
    <br>On http://www.kids-dinosaurs.com/dinosaurs-triceratops.html I found
        some information about the triceratops.
    <br>
    <br>"They lived about 68 to 65 million years ago - in the cretaceous
        period. This was at the same time as some really big meat eating
        dinosaurs such as Tyrannosaurus rex, Albertosaurus and Spinosaurus.
    <br>
    <br>
    <img class="logo" src="http://www.kids-dinosaurs.com/images/xdinosaurs
        -triceratops-facts.png.pagespeed.ic.qbrHGhoMgX.webp" />
    <br>
    <br>To defend itself against meat eaters (predators) it had two long
        brow horns. These could grow to be at least 1 metre (3 feet) long.
        Triceratops would have been able to cause a lot of damage to an
        attacker!
    <br>
    <br>It also had a third shorter horn at the end of its nose. This gives
        it its dinosaur name, which means 'three-horned face'."
</div>
```

If you copy anything from a book or web site, or you got ideas from a book or web site, you should cite your source! That means you are giving credit to that web site or book so that people know that the person who made that web site or book are the ones who came up with that information.

Go to http://www.w3schools.com/tags/ for a guide reference on all the different tags you can use. Notice that in the previous image, there is a new img tag. Try using that one to add more pictures!

2 Go to YouTube.com with an adult's permission and find a video on your topic.

3 Click Share and then Embed. Copy the HTML code with the iframe tag in it by pressing Ctrl+C if you're on Windows and ⌘-C if you're on Mac.

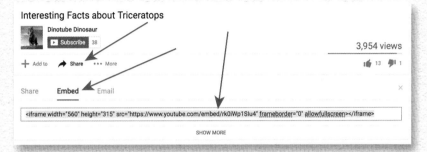

4 Go back to your index.html and delete the text "My right div." Then paste the iframe tag in the right div by pressing Ctrl+V if you're on Windows and ⌘-V if you're on Mac.

```
<div class="right">
    <iframe width="560" height="315" src="https://www.youtube.com
        /embed/rk0iWp1SIu4" frameborder="0" allowfullscreen
        ></iframe>
</div>
```

5 Change width="###" to max-width="100%" and change height="###" to height="auto".

```
<div class="right">
<iframe max-width="100%" height="auto" src="https://www.youtube.com/embed
    /rk0iWp1SIu4" frameborder="0" allowfullscreen></iframe>
</div>
```

CHANGE YOUR FOOTER TEXT

Don't forget to make changes to the text in your footer! Make your footer say something fun, but remember – don't put any information about you. Not even your name.

```
<footer>
    This is my website about dinosaurs.
    <br>
    I learned how to build it from a book!|
</footer>
```

ADD CONTENT TO YOUR OTHER PAGES

You now have the skills to be able to add content to all your other pages! Try making more pages, and even try playing around with the style!

For more information about web site building, you can always check out the wecan.zone/website-building for updated content, videos, and more.

SHARE WITH YOUR FRIENDS

The final thing to do is share your web site! You know how to see your own web site, but the URL is really long and complicated.

1 **Highlight the URL in the address bar and press Ctrl+C if you're on Windows and ⌘-C if you're on Mac to copy it.**

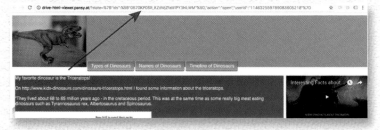

2 **Go to goo.gl. This a web site that takes a long URL and gives it a shorter version that is easier to remember!**

3 **Paste your URL into the URL shortner and click Shorten URL.**

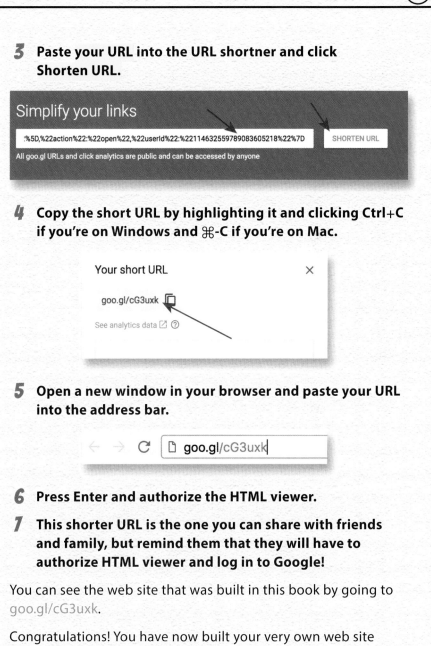

4 **Copy the short URL by highlighting it and clicking Ctrl+C if you're on Windows and ⌘-C if you're on Mac.**

5 **Open a new window in your browser and paste your URL into the address bar.**

6 **Press Enter and authorize the HTML viewer.**

7 **This shorter URL is the one you can share with friends and family, but remind them that they will have to authorize HTML viewer and log in to Google!**

You can see the web site that was built in this book by going to goo.gl/cG3uxk.

Congratulations! You have now built your very own web site using HTML and CSS coding languages!

ABOUT THE AUTHOR

Greg Rickaby is a Lead Front-End Developer at WebDevStudios, a development agency that specializes in creating solutions using WordPress for enterprise-level clients such as Microsoft, Viacom, the Discovery Channel, Uber, Campbell's Soup, and more. He's been writing code for the web since the late 1990s and professionally since 2000. Greg also has a passion for teaching others, contributing to open source technologies, scouting, and being outdoors.

Greg and his beautiful wife, Tara, are the proud parents of Chase, Chloe, and Wyatt. They reside in southern Alabama. *Creating a Web Site* is his first book for Wiley.

DEDICATION

To those who contribute to open source technology: Together we can build great things.

AUTHOR'S ACKNOWLEDGMENTS

First and foremost, I must acknowledge my best friend, Tara. Her tireless efforts last fall allowed me to disappear on the weekends so that I could write this book. I know that being alone with a newborn and two-year old for an entire season isn't the most fun, so thank you, honey bear!

To my editors, Amy, Allison, and Susan, thank you for your patience and understanding while I learned how to write a book. Thank you to Lisa Sabin-Wilson for being my shoulder to cry on when things got tough. And a very special thank you to my dad, who saw the value in personal computers back in the 1980s. He made sure that my brother and I knew how to use them. As he put it, "I didn't have enough to send you to college, so the best I could do was provide you with the technology necessary to make something of yourself." For that, I'm eternally grateful.

And finally, thank you to Dr. Sarah Guthals for jumping in at the last minute to help get this book finished. Her tireless work behind the scenes is appreciated, and I couldn't have finished the book without her. She's also an author of two books for Wiley including *Minecraft Modding For Kids For Dummies* and *Modding Minecraft*. If you're into Minecraft, you should check them out!

PUBLISHER'S ACKNOWLEDGMENTS

Acquisitions Editor: Amy Fandrei

Project and Copy Editor: Susan Christophersen

Technical Editors: Allison Tarr, Drake Kegley

Editorial Assistant: Serena Novosel

Sr. Editorial Assistant: Cherie Case

Production Editor: Vasanth Koilraj

Marketing: Melisa Duffy, Lauren Noens